LEAD ANYWAY

10 Rules for Leading When You Break the Mold

Laurence Paquette

DE G
DE GRUYTER

ISBN 978-3-11-222953-8
ISBN (e-PDF) 978-3-11-222954-5
ISBN (EPUB) 978-3-11-222955-2
DOI https://doi.org/10.1515/9783112229545

Library of Congress Control Number: 2026950621

Bibliographic information published by the Deutsche Nationalbibliothek
The Deutsche Nationalbibliothek lists this publication in the Deutsche Nationalbibliografie; detailed bibliographic data are available on the internet at http://dnb.dnb.de.

De Gruyter and Walter de Gruyter GmbH are part of De Gruyter Brill.
www.degruyterbrill.com

Questions about General Product Safety Regulation:
productsafety@degruyterbrill.com

Cover image: silvae / iStock / Getty Images Plus
Typesetting: Michelle Morgan

LEAD
ANYWAY

*For the ones who learned to adjust their tone
before they learned to trust their voice.
This book is for you.*

"You don't have to be loud to lead". That is the line in Lead Anyway that really stuck with me. This book is inspiring for all of us who don't fit the dominant norms. Laurence gives us the tools and reassurance that we have what it takes to lead - and to lead effectively. A must read!

Dr. Poornima Luthra, senior faculty at Imperial Business School.

In a world that pulls us without asking, Laurence gently brings us back to ourselves. This book is about shifting perspectives, reclaiming intention and becoming the kind of leader who moves others not by force but by authenticity and heart.

Kerstin Knapp, Executive Coaching & Advisory, 360degreepresence.com

FOREWORD

This book is for everyone and anyone who has spent years trying to fit in and struggled throughout this process. If that's you, this book is for you. And if you've started to wonder what could happen if you stopped trying, I strongly urge you to keep reading.

Personally, I didn't set out to become a leader, I only set out to survive and to figure out how to belong in rooms where I never truly felt I should have been in the first place. I set out to make a career to earn money and pay the bills because that's what I had been told. And, to my own surprise, I succeeded. I actually made a career out of being good at things that never felt quite right for me and I've managed to be taken seriously in systems that were never built for people like me. I made a career doubting myself every step of the way, never truly understanding how things worked and trying my best to hide my confusion and discomfort.

For years, I thought that I was the problem. I thought that I was too intense or too anxious or too sensitive. There were times where I thought I was too direct and probably just too different. So I tried to be better, to be "normal". I tried to be more extroverted, more relaxed, and more polished. I thought that was what was needed for leadership and to lead others. I thought it required a version of myself that was more conformist, more charismatic, more confident. I've lost count of how many times I've been in the bathroom during networking events rehearsing small talk I didn't want to have, wishing I could just go home.

So to succeed, I became an extrovert at work (I'm an introvert), I prepared short sentences to always be ready to say something clever in meetings, I laughed at jokes I didn't understand, I mingled, I delivered and I got promoted. I molded myself to what was expected of leaders, I pretended to be confident, decisive and I became someone I wasn't.

While being this corporate version of myself I created to fit in, I started noticing that the leaders I trusted the most weren't necessarily the ones who spoke the loudest or seemed the most sure of themselves. The leaders I trusted were usually the ones who showed up with consistency, who created space for others and who asked really good questions. Those leaders made others feel safe and they did so not by being perfect but simply by being present.

Think of Gandalf, who guided not by showing off, but by being calm and wise, always showing up when it mattered most. If you really think about it, Gandalf doesn't say much, but his silence speaks for itself and through it he creates space for everyone to think and find their own answers and that, to me, is leadership. Or think of Professor McGonagall, whose quiet strength and steady presence earned deep respect without ever needing to show off. These characters don't lead by taking space, they lead by helping others feel safe to take up their own space.

And then I started to wonder and ask myself questions I should have asked myself all along. Does leadership really have to be bold, extroverted, confident? Isn't this version of leadership outdated? Does leadership really demand you look like everyone else and that you fit the mold? Does leadership require that you hide who you are to conform or can you not lead from the margins with empathy and honesty?

Can you not lead anyway?

And the answer is yes. You can lead anyway. You can lead by being yourself even when you don't fit the mold.

Therefore, I decided to write this book you hold in your hands. I wrote it for the quiet ones, the late bloomers, the neurodiverse, the socially anxious, the overthinkers, the high-masking autistic professionals and for everyone who feels too much and tries too hard.

In short, this book is for anyone who's ever sat in a meeting thinking *"Am I the only one not getting this?"* Let's be honest, how many of us have sat in a meeting and wondered what was really being discussed. And I wrote this book for those of us who've learned to mask how much effort it takes to just keep up.

As you might expect, this is a book about leadership, but not the kind that rewards dominance or performance. There are no quick hacks or solve-it-all formulas in this book. There are no immediate fixes or shortcuts, because there shouldn't be. We shouldn't strive to try to be like everyone else, we should strive to be ourselves. This book is about lived experience, tools that work, and stories that might sound like yours.

What you'll find in these pages are ten rules and practical tools shaped by lived experiences, my own and others. These rules come from leading inside systems that weren't designed for people like me and from years of noticing what actually helps people thrive in the business world, regardless of who they are as people. These pages are rooted in real life, but they are also backed by research as I've drawn from psychology, neuroscience, leadership theory, and workplace studies to reinforce what my own story kept teaching me over the years: that being quiet, that being different, and that being honest about who we are don't have to be barriers to leadership. On the contrary, they can be the source of it.

My hope is that this book gives you permission to lead as you are, to stop performing, to trust your own presence and to take up space, in your own way. You're not broken and you don't need fixing. You don't need to turn yourself into someone else and you don't need to keep waiting until you feel ready.

You can lead anyway.

Let's begin.

INTRODUCTION

"We don't see things as they are, we see them as we are."
Anaïs Nin

The book you're holding right now isn't a traditional leadership book.

This book doesn't include formulas, a five-step plan to fix everything, there's no advice on how to dominate the room or "win" at work (whatever that means?). Instead, this book is a guide for leading on your own terms, especially if you've spent most of your career trying to fit into a system that never felt designed for you.

The rules outlined in this book were born from lived experience. They come from leading while being neurodivergent, while being an introvert and while leading through burnout, grief, masking and self-doubt. These rules were shaped in real meetings facing real pressure and inside corporate cultures that didn't always make space for being different.

These rules are also grounded in research and throughout this book, you'll find insights from psychology, neuroscience, leadership theory and various studies on workplace and corporate environments. This book isn't a memoir or a list of tips, but hopefully a guide that can help others navigate the business world with more ease. I hope this book will be a bridge between personal truth and professional growth for anyone who's ever questioned whether they were too quiet, too intense or too unsure to lead.

The book is divided into three parts:

PART 1: WHO WE ARE

Before we lead others, we need to understand ourselves.
This section explores identity, being different, self-doubt, and the internal stories we carry about what leadership is supposed to look like.

- Rule 1: You Don't Have to Be Loud to Lead
- Rule 2: Your Weird Is Your Superpower
- Rule 3: You Feel Like an Impostor

PART 2: HOW WE LEAD

Once we stop trying to fit the mold, we can build leadership from a more grounded place.

This section is about mindset, tools, and protecting your energy as you lead from the margins.

- Rule 4: Ask Better Questions
- Rule 5: Boundaries Are Culture
- Rule 6: Burnout Is Not a Badge of Honor
- Rule 7: Grieve and Lead at the Same Time

PART 3: CHANGING THE GAME

Leadership isn't just about fitting in, it's about creating change.

This final section invites you to redefine success, take up space, and lead in ways that challenge outdated norms.

- Rule 8: Success Has No Expiry Date
- Rule 9: You Don't Need Permission
- Rule 10: Lead Anyway

Each of the 10 rules stands alone and you don't need to read them in order. Start where you need to, whether it's with burnout, boundaries, or something else.

PART 1 – WHO WE ARE

"To be great is to be misunderstood"
Ralph Waldo Emerson

Are you a quiet overthinker finding yourself sitting in a room full of fast talkers and colleagues that love noisy brainstorms or quick ping pong decisions? Do you need time to process your thoughts while everyone around you seems to thrive on being spontaneous? Have you spent years of your life masking parts of who you are and hiding your sensitivity, your intensity or your anxiety just to blend in?

Maybe you've been told that you're too quiet in one setting and too direct in another, too sensitive one day and too bold the next as if no version of you is ever quite right. Maybe you've learned to play along and by this I mean that you've learned to nod along, to smile when expected, and to act like everything was fine, even when you're unraveling inside. Maybe you've laughed at a joke you didn't find funny or didn't even understand or forced yourself to small talk until your social battery was completely depleted. And finally, maybe you've always felt like leadership wasn't built for people like you.

If that's you, you're not alone.

Before we can lead others, we have to learn how to lead ourselves. Not the version that shows up to impress in a performance review, but the real one caught between our true identity and the expectations of what leadership is supposed to look like.

This first section of the book is about the quiet battles that happen before any big decisions are made. The thoughts that race through your head in a meeting while others are discussing and you're trying to figure out if, how and when you should jump in. This section is about the way your heart sinks when everyone else seems louder or more confident than you. And maybe most importantly, it's about those moments when you wonder if you're just faking it better than most and no one notices you don't fit the mold.

This first section is also about the parts of yourself you've been told to dial down: your introversion, your sensitivity, your awkwardness or your difference. All these parts and quirks you have that make you feel like you're too much or not enough or both at once. It's also about the parts you've hidden in order to blend in, especially if you're neurodivergent, anxious or just wired a little differently.

Leadership starts here. It doesn't start with a title or with performance. It starts with self-awareness, with presence and with the decision to stop becoming someone else just to be taken seriously.

This is where we begin: by unlearning what leadership is supposed to look like, and remembering who we are underneath it all. Especially if who you are never fits the mold.

Rule 1: You Don't Have to Be Loud to Lead

"There's zero correlation between being the best talker and having the best ideas."
Susan Cain

I used to dread introductions. Actually, I still do most of the time.

We all have encountered those moments in workshops or team offsites when you're supposed to say your name, your role, and something fun about yourself. You know, the icebreakers at the networking dinners or at the business events where everyone seems to be effortlessly confident, funny, magnetic and always ready with something clever to say.

I used to sit and watch the charismatic people speak. You know, the loud, energetic ones who have the blessing of being comfortable in their own skin, a feeling I've yet to fully understand. And while watching them I'd simply feel like I didn't belong. I wasn't shy or afraid of people, I just wasn't *that*. While others joked easily about their hobbies or pets or football, I sat there overthinking every possible answer to the question "what's fun about me", trying to sound interesting, memorable, and just *"normal"* enough. My brain would freeze, I didn't light up the room and I didn't have the energy to be "on" all the time. Instead, I was thoughtful, focused, and anxious. Quiet, and very anxious.

For a while, I believed that meant I wasn't cut out for leadership. I believed I needed to become someone else to succeed, especially in the corporate world. Someone more charismatic, someone more likable, more fun, more outgoing, more extroverted and more capable of speaking spontaneously without overthinking every thought.

So I studied the charismatic people I came across. And when I say I studied, I really did. I took notes on how they spoke, how they moved, how they used their hands and how they laughed at the right moments. And based on my studies, I trained myself to be more outgoing, to smile more than I wanted to and to laugh even when I didn't think it was funny. I even learned to interrupt conversations just to sound confident and to learn how to fake certainty. I prepared clever introductions in advance, I learned how to drop punchlines and soundbites like I wasn't rehearsing them in my head all morning. And by doing so, I started performing leadership instead of practicing it.

But eventually the performance started to wear me down. By 2020, in the middle of the pandemic, I hit a wall. The back to back Teams calls, pretending to be a leader I wasn't and the pressure to project a polished, charismatic version of myself, while sitting in my own office/bedroom collided into a reality I couldn't sustain. As the pandemic forced me to work from home a lot, being my made up *"work self"* in my house drained me completely. I think it hit me hard because home used to be my safe place where I allowed myself to be just me without pretending and now having to work from home full time, I could no longer be myself in my own home. The mask I had worn at work for years was already becoming unbearable before the pandemic, but it accelerated the crash. At first, I told myself I was just tired, but deep down I knew I was burned out. Not from the job itself but from all the pretending it was requiring from me.

This was the turning point.

And slowly, very slowly, something in me started to rebel. First, it was very quiet, I almost didn't notice. But over time, I started to hear this voice that said: What if I just stopped trying to be someone else? What if I tried to be more myself and do what feels right to me?

I didn't act on this thought right away. Not at all. I was way too scared and I didn't want to risk the career I had spent years building. But by 2022, that voice had grown louder and when I got promoted to Vice President, leading the Global Marketing team at the company I worked at, I felt a shift. The shift was probably due to the fact that I had attained a corporate level I never imagined I'd reach and I didn't expect to climb any higher. After spending years proving that I belonged, I now felt I had reached a level where I wanted to belong on my own terms. I now wanted to lead, not by mimicking others, but by being more myself.

What I thought for years were weaknesses, my quietness, my steadiness, my ability to read the room in an instant, my need to reflect before I speak, my discomfort with performative leadership, I realized were actually the things that made me effective. I didn't need to become more charismatic, I needed to become more honest, more grounded. More me.

What We Have Been Taught About Leadership

Most of us were taught that leaders are supposed to be bold, magnetic, and extroverted. That leaders are present and visible and that presence means walking into a room and making sure everyone notices you. Most of us are taught that confidence looks like fast answers, firm handshakes, and the ability to speak without notes.

This version of leadership is everywhere: on stage, on LinkedIn and in corporate training programs. It's the loud voice that gets credited for the team's success, it's the person who interrupts and dominates the meeting and somehow gets rewarded for being *"assertive"*. This version of leadership rewards performance and fast pace. It favors those who speak first, even if they have the least to say or have the shallowest input to share. Loudness is often perceived as more valuable than the depth of the input.

And for these reasons, I don't wonder why so many of us believe we're not cut out for leadership. It's no wonder we stay quiet in meetings even when we have something to say. We second-guess ourselves when we need a pause to think, because the model we have been shown tells us that "real" leaders always have instant answers. Over time, we learn to perform rather than contribute, to fit the mold instead of bringing what makes us different.

Susan Cain, in *Quiet*, puts it simply and argues that there's zero correlation between being the best talker and having the best ideas. And yet, in most workplaces, we still equate leadership with speaking up quickly and often.[1]

If you're quiet, thoughtful, neurodivergent, socially anxious, or simply uninterested in pretending to be someone you're not, it can feel like leadership is a game you're not built to play nor win. But here is the truth: leadership isn't about charisma and it's not about being loud. Leadership is about trust, it's about clarity and it's about being able to show up and create safety, direction and momentum for others. Charisma can help, but it's not required.

Take the example of Satya Nadella, the CEO of Microsoft. It's not in his nature to take the most prominent spot in the room or to be the loudest speaker. Listening intently and making room for others are the two qualities that define him. As a result of his leadership, Microsoft's culture shifted from internal rivalry to collaboration, and the company grew stronger. His influence shows that presence isn't about performance, it's about clarity, empathy, and trust.[2]

Harvard Business Review has written extensively about the power of quiet leaders. One study found that introverted leaders often deliver better outcomes, especially when they lead proactive teams, because they're more likely to listen and support others' ideas rather than push their own, which is often problematic in the business world, where leaders believe they have the best ideas and don't take the time to listen to the team's input.[3]

Leadership requires presence and unlike popular belief, presence isn't about grabbing attention and it's not about dazzling people. It's about offering your full attention and it's about grounding the people you lead. And you can absolutely do that while being a quiet leader and not a great charismatic figure.

In fact, many charismatic leaders are great at captivating an audience but terrible at holding space. They can inspire in a keynote, yet forget to check in after a meeting. They speak loudly, but don't always listen. They share ideas, but overlook other people's contributions.

I've been led by these personas. Leaders who are magnetic in front of a crowd and make everyone believe, briefly, in their vision. But outside those performances, they struggle to be present. They don't really see the people they lead and they don't create safety.

In my view, although we often call them leaders, they are not leading. They are skilled orators, capable of sprinkling a little fairy dust on an audience, but unable to sustain trust once the spotlight fades.

Over the years, I've learned that some of the strongest leaders I know don't perform leadership, they live it. And they do so quietly, consistently and authentically.

So if you've ever felt like you're not visible enough, not dynamic enough, not outgoing enough, I want you to hear this clearly: you're not disqualified, you're not behind and you're not broken. You simply have not yet been taught that your kind of leadership is valuable. It is and we need more of it.

Redefining Presence and Confidence

Presence is one of those words that gets thrown around in leadership conversations, often without a clear definition:

"She has presence."

"He really owns the room."

"They're so magnetic."

But what does this actually mean?

For a long time, I thought presence was about being seen more than others. I believed presence came from being loud, being active in all conversations, talking more than anyone else and always having something to say. You were present if you were a confident speaker and if you were a person who walks in the room and commands attention. And of course, if that's what presence meant, I firmly believed I didn't have any as I don't like to be perceived and I like to walk quietly into rooms without being noticed.

Over time, I realized presence isn't about volume or visibility. It doesn't come from filling every silence or commanding every room. Presence can be quiet, steady, and grounded. It's not about taking up space, it's about creating space where others feel seen and heard.

Amy Cuddy, a social psychologist at Harvard, redefined the concept beautifully in her book *Presence* where she argues that presence isn't about pretending to be competent; it's about believing in and revealing the abilities you truly have. [4]

I used to sit in meetings thinking I needed to speak more, that I needed to show I was engaged or that I needed to sound more assertive. I'd prepare mental bullet points just in case someone called on me. You know that moment where someone unexpectedly says *"what about you, what do you think?"*. Personally, I have a lot of thoughts and opinions but being called on the spot freezes me and I become a complete mute. All my thoughts vanish and I find it extremely hard to say something intelligent. So for that reason, I'd rehearse clever things to say, how to say them and what tone to use to make sure I wouldn't sound rude or cold or too direct. And I'd prepare thoroughly not just to contribute but to prove that I belonged in the room. It was stressful, exhausting and most importantly, it was fake. I didn't speak from presence, I spoke from fear.

Presence doesn't have to be loud and to prove my point, let's look at an example. In 1955, in Montgomery, Alabama, public buses were segregated by law. Black passengers were required to give up their seats to white passengers when asked. When Rosa Parks, a Black seamstress and civil rights activist, was told to stand so a white man could sit, she refused. She didn't raise her voice, she didn't make a speech and she didn't try to persuade anyone in the moment. She simply stayed seated.

That quiet act of defiance led to her arrest and helped spark the Montgomery Bus Boycott, a year long mass protest that became a turning point in the American civil rights movement. Her presence wasn't passive, it was deliberate. It came from clarity and it led to real, structural change. Rosa Parks showed that presence can be quiet and powerful.

I began to see this in my own way too, at a much smaller and far less consequential scale. When I stopped performing and simply paid attention and I mean *really* paid attention, I noticed a shift. I only spoke when I had something intentional to say, and people started to listen more. Not because I was talking a lot, but because when I did speak, it came from clarity, reflection, and care.

It also gave me permission not to talk. When people asked me out of the blue, *"What do you think, Laurence?"* or called on me in a meeting, I became comfortable saying, *"I don't know yet. I'm still collecting my thoughts."* And it's surprising how much people respect the answer *"I don't know."*

Once, after a long meeting, someone from the team messaged me privately and said, *"I always wait for your take. It's usually the thing that helps me make sense of the rest."* This stayed with me. It reminded me that I didn't have to be loud to be heard. I just had to be present and speak when it mattered.

It also made me realize something important. I've been in so many meetings where buzzwords fly and people speak so quickly and spontaneously that I lose track of what we're even trying to solve. And in those moments, I used to panic. I worried that my brain couldn't keep up and my impostor syndrome kicked in hard. I worried that my cognitive abilities weren't sharp enough to belong in the room. But overtime, I've since learned something important: if I don't understand what's going on, chances are, most of the people in the room feel the same way. They're just too afraid to say it.

In short, to be present, you don't have to *"own the room"*. Instead, you can ground the room. You don't have to speak quickly or think out loud in front of everyone to prove your worth or that you belong. You can pause, you can reflect, you can ask better questions. Presence isn't about being performative, but it's about being fully here in the moment.

Leadership researcher Kristi Hedges defines presence as the quality that enables a leader to connect with, influence and inspire others through how they show up and communicate.[5] That connection doesn't come from volume, but it comes from alignment, from presence that feels steady, not performative. It's the ability to make people feel seen without needing to be seen first. It's the energy that helps others settle down, feel safe and find clarity.

This kind of presence isn't only valid, it's powerful. Especially in a world that's loud, hyper reactive and constantly moving. Being someone who brings clarity and steadiness isn't just a leadership style, it's a leadership advantage.

One of the most damaging myths about leadership is that confidence is either something you're born with or you're not. This myth tells us that confidence is a fixed trait, a personality characteristic and a natural gift. But is it?

I once heard in a TV show called *Euphoria* one of the characters say *"90 percent of life is confidence. And the thing about confidence is no one knows if it's real or not."* By saying this, the character points out that so much of how people succeed, get noticed or are treated often comes down less to actual skills or competence and more on how confidently they present themselves. Confidence changes how people see you. But the thing about confidence is that no one knows if it's real or not. No one knows if the person exhibiting confidence is faking it or really confident. To others, the appearance of confidence is often as powerful whether it's genuine or not.

Now, I'm not saying we should all fake confidence. That's a hard and taxing activity, but what I want to say is that the myth that confidence is something you either have or not is completely false and it keeps too many capable people from stepping into leadership. Especially people who overthink, second-guess themselves, feel like they need to be 100 percent ready before they speak or feel that they don't fit the typical corporate mold.

And here is what everyone should know: confidence isn't a personality trait. It's a skill. It's something you can learn, build, practice, rehearse and strengthen. And like any skill, it grows through repetition, not perfection. And over time you can actually become confident.

Social psychologist Albert Bandura, one of the most influential researchers on motivation and learning, called this *self-efficacy*: the belief in your ability to succeed in specific situations.[6] He showed that people develop confidence not from success alone, but from small experiences of mastery over time. Confidence comes from doing, from trying and when failing, from getting back up.

And yet, in corporate culture, we often confuse confidence with charisma. We assume the loudest person in the room must also be the most certain. But volume isn't proof of certainty and certainty isn't the same as clarity.

In her book *Radical Candor*[7], Kim Scott warns against what she calls *"ruinous empathy"* and *"obnoxious aggression"* in leaders who speak boldly but without emotional intelligence. Her message is clear: confidence without care isn't leadership, it's actually performance.

Real confidence is grounded, it can be quiet, it can be calm and it doesn't have to dominate others. It can hold space not just for yourself but for others and for nuance. Real confidence doesn't fear being wrong or being contested. That kind of confidence isn't about knowing everything, it's about trusting yourself enough to show up anyway. It's about knowing when to speak and when to listen and it's about knowing when you need time to reflect and when you don't have the answers.

Many of us, including myself, used to think that we have to be bulletproof before we can speak. That if we're unsure, we should stay quiet and that confidence means being certain. But if we really think about it, we realize that people trust us more when we speak with humility and show that we're still learning.

Now, instead of trying to be bulletproof, I say things like:

"I'm still figuring this out, but here's what I think." Or *"I'm open to being wrong, let's explore this further."* And when I do, people listen more closely, not less.

In short, confidence isn't loud and it's not about never hesitating. Confidence is about choosing to show up, even when you feel unsure, confidence is speaking with intent and not just volume. Confidence is saying *"I don't have all the answers, but I'm here"*. And that's what makes you trustworthy and that's what makes you a leader.

Tips and Tools: You Don't Have to Be Loud to Lead

If you've spent years trying to act more confident, sound more extroverted, or speak more quickly, I want to offer another way forward. You don't need to perform leadership to be a leader, you just need to be intentional about how you show up.

Presence isn't about changing who you are. It's about learning how to bring more of yourself into the room and to do so with purpose.

Here are five practices that can help you to lead powerfully without pretending.

1. Anchor Yourself

Before you walk into a meeting, deliver a presentation, or start a difficult conversation, pause.

Breathe.

Feel your feet on the ground.

Notice your spine, your breath, your presence in the room.

This may sound simple, but it's one of the most effective tools we have to anchor ourselves into the moment.

For many of us, especially those who are neurodivergent, anxious, or highly sensitive, our nervous systems can become overstimulated quickly. We start performing instead of showing up and we lose ourselves in the rush to seem confident. Grounding is how we come back to ourselves.

Dr. Lisa Feldman Barrett, a neuroscientist and author of *How Emotions Are Made*, explains that our brains are constantly guessing what's going to happen next. If we ground ourselves, we can help our brains guess better.[8]

That's what anchoring does, it gives your body and your brain a reference point and it calms your internal signals so you can be present with others. And when you're calm and grounded, people feel that.

I've had moments where I've been on stage or about to join a high-stakes meeting, and everything in me felt wired. My brain was spinning, my heart was racing, my jaw was clenched. Anchoring myself for even 10 seconds reset my nervous system and it calmed me down. It helped me be more in the moment and that's what people respond to, presence.

Here's another way to anchor yourself in the moment and something you can do anywhere without anyone noticing.

- Take a slow inhale while you count to four.
- Hold your breath for two seconds.
- Exhale while you count to six.
- Feel your feet on the floor.
- Repeat once or twice.

This signals to your body that you're safe, that you're not being chased, that you don't need to perform to survive and that you're here, in the moment.

And if you feel that doing this, that having to anchor yourself makes you less professional, it doesn't. It's not weak or unprofessional to take a moment to ground yourself. It makes you more available to think clearly, hold space and lead with intent.

2. Own the Pause

Most of us are taught to fear silence. As children in classrooms, the fastest hand in the air or the person who speaks first is rewarded. Being quick to answer is praised and therefore so many of us learn to fill up silence rather than sit with it. Silence is also often misread in conversations as ignorance or disinterest or disagreement. People rush to fill silence to avoid being misunderstood. And in hierarchical workplaces, especially in the west, silence is often mistaken for a lack of confidence or a lack of competences.

But silence, when used with intention, signals presence and authority. Think of some of the most impactful speakers you've ever heard. They pause. They let words land. They're not in a rush to fill the air. And those pauses they make, they're not awkward, they're powerful.

If you're looking for good examples of this, I suggest you watch Barack Obama's victory speech from 2008. In this speech, he uses deliberate pauses after short and simple sentences. This silence amplified what he said and gave people the opportunity to own and savour the moment. Steve Jobs did the same in his commencement address at Stanford University in 2005. He spoke slowly and paused often, especially when moving between stories. He also used silence after saying "Stay hungry. Stay foolish." That pause allowed the words to sink in and land with force. And finally, if you need a third example, Greta Thunberg also uses silence often to make moments more powerful and even uncomfortable as a way to engage and impact the audience. At the UN Climate Action Summit in 2019, she used her silence after saying "How dare you!" forcing the audience to sit with the weight of what she just had said.

Silence and pauses are not awkward if they are used with intent. In those cases, they can be extremely powerful. It tells the room, I'm not rushing, I'm thinking or I'm leaving you with this thought for you to consider. It gives your words space to breathe and for others to process them.

And when you pause before responding, breathing in and taking a few seconds, you're not showing uncertainty. You're showing that you're considering what matters and that changes how people listen. In a world of instant replies and constant noise and movement, a thoughtful pause before speaking up can make others lean in and this shouldn't be underestimated.

Executive coach Nancy Kline, in *Time to Think*, writes that *"The quality of everything we do depends on the quality of the thinking we do first. And the quality of that thinking depends on the way we treat each other while we are thinking."* [9] That includes giving ourselves space to think before we speak.

In my own leadership journey, I've found that when I pause before speaking, especially in high-stakes meetings, it does more than calm me, it signals confidence. It slows the tempo of the room and in turns, it lets others breathe, too.

If you struggle with overthinking or feel pressure to respond quickly, try this: when someone asks a question, take one full breath before answering. You'll notice that people wait, they'll lean in and that pause becomes your power, not your liability.

3. Speak When It Matters

You don't need to talk constantly to be seen as a leader, instead you just need to make your words count.

In many corporate settings, especially fast-paced or extrovert-driven ones, there's an unspoken pressure to jump in often, to comment on every update, to be the first to have an opinion.

Some of the most effective leaders I've worked with were not the ones who talked the most, but they were the ones who knew when to speak and made people pause when they did. They listened deeply, reflected quietly, and when they finally shared something, it shifted the energy in the room.

This is especially powerful for those of us who process slowly, internally, or prefer listening over performing. Our contributions often come with nuance, thoughtfulness, and clarity, but for that to work, we have to trust that value doesn't lie in volume.

A Harvard Business School study on communication in teams found that speaking less, but at the right time, can significantly increase your influence and perceived leadership effectiveness.[10] In other words: when you say something that helps the room move forward, even if it's brief, people notice.

Try these simple tricks:

- Instead of thinking *"What should I say?"* try *"What needs to be said?"*
- If you feel pressure to speak, pause and ask yourself, *"Will this add clarity or just fill space?"*

- If something meaningful is said and you agree, reinforce it by mentioning it again and crediting the person who said it in the first place. You don't need a brand-new idea to show leadership. We often forget that alignment and amplification matter too.

People don't remember who talked the most, they remember who made the conversation smarter, kinder, clearer, or more focused.

4. Lead Through Questions

Rule 4 of this book focuses on asking questions and how it can help you be a better leader, but asking questions can also help you to be more present. Presence isn't just about making bold declarations, but it's also about asking the kind of questions that make people think more clearly.

In fact, some of the most impactful leaders I've seen don't speak in statements, they speak in questions. And they do so not because they lack direction, but because they understand that real leadership isn't about having all the answers. It's about helping the team find better ones together.

This is especially powerful for introverts, reflective thinkers, and neurodivergent leaders who may need more time to process before speaking. Asking the right question can cut through noise and re-anchor the room, while it can clarify a conversation, challenge assumptions, and unlock new insight.

Edgar Schein, a pioneer in organizational development, wrote extensively about this in *Humble Inquiry*, where he shows that real influence is built not by telling people what to do, but by creating space for collaborative discovery. As he argues throughout the book, telling puts us in control, while asking builds relationships and opens the door to real help."[11]

So how do you lead through questions?

- Ask clarifying questions like *"What problem are we actually trying to solve?"* or *"What does success look like here?"*
- Ask alignment questions like *"What do we all agree on?"* or *"Where are we not yet aligned?"*
- Ask curiosity-based questions like *"What have we not considered yet?"* or *"Who else should we include in this decision?"*

Leading through questions isn't passive, to the contrary. It shows you're not just thinking about what's being said, you're thinking about how people are thinking.

5. Let Your Body Speak

You don't need big gestures or exaggerated energy to have presence, but your body is always speaking and in leadership, people are always listening.

When you enter a room or log onto a call, your physical presence shapes how others perceive you and how you feel about yourself. A slouched posture, darting eyes, or fidgeting may not reflect how capable you are but they often reflect how safe or grounded you feel in the moment.

Amy Cuddy's research[4] found that posture can significantly influence both self-perception and external perception. She explains that our body language can reinforce the belief that we belong in the room, not just to others, but to ourselves.

Letting your body speak doesn't mean faking boldness, it means aligning your posture with the energy you want to bring:

- Sit fully in your chair, without perching or shrinking. Use the chair to your advantage and feel its support.
- Place your feet flat on the ground to feel anchored.
- Relax your shoulders and your jaw. Tension in the body often signals emotional overwhelm.
- Look up occasionally, scan the room and make eye contact when and if it feels right.

You don't need to be theatrical, but when you embody calm, confidence, and curiosity, even just through posture and calm breathing, others will feel it and the best part is that so will you.

Presence isn't a trick, it's a practice and the more you do it the better you become at it.

And remember, the goal is never to become someone else. It is to be yourself, in a way that allows people to trust you, follow you, and feel safe around you, without you ever needing to be a bold extroverted leader.

Visual Summary

Practice	What It Looks Like	Why It Works
1. Anchor Yourself	Take a deep breath. Feel your feet. Ground your body.	Regulates your nervous system and sets a calm, steady tone.
2. Own the Pause	Stop talking. Take time to pause. Let silence do its job	Builds authority and gives space for ideas to land.
3. Speak When It Matters	Focus on clarity over quantity. Make your words count.	Increases your perceived influence and trustworthiness.
4. Lead Through Questions	Ask thoughtful, intentional questions.	Encourages collaboration, connection, and reflection.
5. Let Your Body Speak	Sit fully. Loosen your jaw. Make eye contact when it feels right.	Reinforces presence and confidence, internally and externally.

Micro-Practice: The Power Pause

To internalize new learnings, micro changes can help drive adoption and help incorporate in our daily practices new learnings. For this reason, I firmly believe in micro-practices. These are small, deliberate adjustments that help what we learn settle into how we act, without changing who we are.

For rule 1, I suggest the following micro practice. In your next meeting, do this one thing:

Every time you speak, pause for two full seconds before you speak. That's it.

You can count to yourself or you can breathe through it. And it's ok to let it feel a little awkward and still, don't rush to fill the silence.

That pause will do several things:

- It gives your brain space to find the right words.
- It signals calm and confidence to others.
- It invites the room to slow down and listen.

Try it once and then try it again. Over time, this small practice builds a quiet kind of presence that people start to trust instinctively.

Practical Quick Phrases

Sometimes the hardest part of showing presence and confidence is knowing what to say in the moment. If you're like me, you may find comfort in having a few ready-made phrases you can lean on. I use pre-made sentences all the time as anchor points and quick go-tos to help me navigate difficult conversations and help me be able to respond on the spot, something I struggle with otherwise. These aren't scripts to follow word for word, but quick anchors you can use to pause, buy yourself time, or show confidence without having to perform.

- *"Let me pause a moment before I respond."*
- *"I don't have the full answer right now, but I'll get back to you."*
- *"I would love to hear from others before I share my view."*
- *"I need a moment to gather my thoughts."*
- *"I may not know everything, but I can speak to what I've seen so far."*
- *"I'm still processing, but here's where I'm at right now."*

Checklist: What Will You Try This Week?

This checklist is not about doing everything at once. Choose one small thing to try this week and notice what shifts when you give yourself a little more space to be present.

- Take a breath and ground yourself before entering the room
- Give yourself permission to pause instead of rushing to respond
- Speak when you have something intentional to say
- Ask at least one thoughtful question to guide or deepen the conversation
- Pay attention to your posture and physical presence (no shrinking, no faking)
- Embrace silence as part of communication
- Try one of the quick phrases suggested

Closing: Presence Over Performance

Presence doesn't come from being the loudest person in the room. It doesn't come from dominating the conversation, telling the best story, or projecting confidence at all costs. Presence comes from how you inhabit a moment. From whether you are paying attention, from whether your words are intentional, from whether people feel seen, heard, and safe when you are there. Leadership doesn't require charisma or extroversion. It requires steadiness, it requires clarity and it requires the courage to show up without performing.

You can lead quietly, you can lead steadily and you can lead intentionally.

The world doesn't need more leaders who talk constantly and over other people. It needs more leaders who listen, think, and act with purpose. So if you've ever questioned whether you were too quiet to lead, let this be your answer:

You're not too quiet, or too different or missing something to be a leader.

You're already enough, you're just building the skill of showing up as yourself with intent. And that's leadership and it starts here.

Frances Frei, professor at Harvard Business School, teaches that trust, the foundation of strong leadership, is built through a combination of authenticity, logic, and empathy. When those three are present, people follow. As she explains in her work, leaders build trust by being authentic, grounding their ideas in logic, and leading with empathy, even at scale.[12]

Dr. Tomas Chamorro-Premuzic, a psychologist and leadership researcher, has shown that humility and self-awareness are often more predictive of long-term leadership success than charm or overconfidence. Throughout his work, he argues that the most effective leaders are those who recognize their limitations and keep learning, rather than those who are convinced of their own greatness.[13]

I once sat in a chaotic strategy meeting, the kind many of us know all too well. Everyone was talking over one another, throwing ideas all hoping to say something clever that would stick. In that meeting, through all the noise, one of my colleagues stayed completely silent. She was almost always quiet in meetings. That day, she waited. She let the energy burn itself out and slowly the ideas stopped flying and the room finally slowed down. And then she spoke and she asked one short, direct question: *"Are we solving this for us or for the people who will actually use the platform?"* The room fell silent and people looked at each other. It was clear, we had been solving this for ourselves, not for our customers. And just like that, we had a direction.

Later, I pulled her aside and said, *"That question you asked, that's what we needed."* and I thanked her for it and for daring to speak so honestly in such chaos. She thanked me, humbly. It was clear it had taken her a lot of courage to ask the question and insert herself into the room, but her quiet leadership shifted the entire discussion. She gave us clarity and her way of carrying herself stayed with me. It stayed with me because she showed presence, not performance like all the others. And it reminded me that you don't have to take up more space to matter, you just have to be brave enough to take your space fully, honestly and calmly. That's leadership and it's one all of us carry inside ourselves.

Rule 2: Your Weird Is Your Superpower

"The world needs all kinds of minds."
Temple Grandin

We celebrate innovation, creativity, and bold ideas and then we tell people to stop being *"too much"*. We say we value different perspectives, but only if they're delivered in the right tone, at the right time, in the right format. We claim to want diversity of thought, but we reward those who blend in, not the ones who challenge the flow of a meeting or ask the tough questions.

In corporate environments, we often hire for curiosity, intensity, and attention to detail and then coach people to dial those traits down so they fit the corporate expectations and don't over challenge corporate culture and hierarchy. We talk about diversity and its importance, we tell people to bring their full selves to work, while quietly rewarding conformity and asking people to dress appropriately, behave correctly and embrace company values. The unwritten rules are clear: you can be different, but not disruptive. You can be passionate, but not too intense. You can be honest, but not too direct. You can be yourself, as long as it's palatable.

This tension is especially real for neurodivergent professionals, who process the world differently. Psychologist Devon Price calls this the *"camouflage cost"*[14], describing the emotional, cognitive, and physiological toll of constantly trying to pass as neurotypical. Masking, the learned behavior of hiding or suppressing traits to fit in, becomes so automatic that we begin to believe our real selves are the problem.

If you've never heard of masking, let me take a moment to explain what it is. Masking is when people consciously or unconsciously hide parts of who they are to avoid standing out or being judged. It is common among neurodivergent people, but it also shows up in introverts, caregivers, people from marginalized groups, and anyone who has learned that fitting in feels safer than being fully themselves.

Masking can look like changing your tone of voice, forcing eye contact, copying the behavior of others, laughing at things that don't feel funny, or holding back your real reactions. It can help you get by in environments that don't always welcome differences. But over time, it is exhausting. It drains energy, creates distance from yourself, and slowly erodes self-trust.

And for many of us, masking and trying to fit in the corporate world makes us believe that our differences are a liability. Sociologist Marianne

Cooper has shown how organizations continue to reward a narrow prototype of leadership, typically extroverted, assertive, quick on their feet, and socially fluent. When you don't match that mold, your competence is more likely to be questioned and your contributions more likely to be overlooked.[15]

I know this dynamic intimately. I've spent years trying to soften the parts of myself that felt uncomfortable or out of place. I've tried to hide the way my brain works, I've masked my social discomfort and social awkwardness and I did all I could to appear more easygoing, less intense, less sensitive and more agreeable.

I've taught myself to make eye contact by alternating between the other person's right and left eye, looking at one, then the other, back and forth, silently counting the seconds until it felt *"right"* to look away. In truth, I prefer online meetings, because in this setting I don't have to look anyone in the eyes and instead I can focus on my own facial expressions.

In face to face meetings, I listen and I think best when I doodle or look at the table while I speak. Sadly, that kind of behavior is often read as disengagement, not as leadership. So I've learned to stop doodling and to look up. I've also learned not to fidget, or if I do, to do it in ways no one can see. In secret, I curl my toes inside my shoes repeatedly. For a long time, I believed this was what professionalism required. That the cost of belonging was losing parts of myself along the way.

But I've learned, slowly, and sometimes painfully, that the parts of me I used to call weird are the parts that make me effective, that give me an edge and that allow me to lead authentically. The things I once tried to fix or hide are the exact things that have allowed me to lead with clarity, empathy, and vision.

That's the paradox: your weird is your superpower. The quirks, the sensitivities, and the differences you've been told to erase are often the very traits that make you sharper, more empathetic, and more resilient as a leader. They're not weaknesses to cover up, they are the source of your strength.

Greta Thunberg is an excellent example of how traits that are often criticized as *"too much"* can become a source of power. Since she began her activism, she was labeled by critics as overly intense, socially clumsy, too blunt and even weird. Critics condemned and joked on her account that she didn't smile enough, that she was too forceful, and that she was speaking the same desperate message over and over. What they were really reacting to was her refusal to perform the polished, charismatic style of leadership they were accustomed to.

Basically, this was the aspect that made Greta so powerful. She didn't diminish her words to sound acceptable or pleasant, she didn't fake charisma to make people comfortable, and she didn't soften her intensity to blend in. Her focus, her blunt honesty, and even her discomfort with social rules and rituals became the very things that gave her presence and credibility. Millions of people around the world listened because she spoke with clarity and urgency, not because she tried to appear charming or conventional.

Greta's story shows the core truth of this rule: the things that others perceive as faults are really the ones holding the most power. Her so-called *"weirdness"* wasn't a weakness to be concealed, but rather the reason people paid attention to her in the first place.

Psychologist Scott Barry Kaufman, in his research on creativity and nonconformity[16], describes how many of the world's most original thinkers show signs of neurodivergence: ADHD, autism, or high sensitivity, not in spite of their success, but as part of the cognitive diversity that drives it. What a system and many people call a deficit is often a different way to process information and view the world and that can be a superpower.

For me, just like for many others, *"weird"* can take on multiple forms and shape and change day by day. It can be to struggle to concentrate because the lights in the office are too bright or to be incapable of following the conversation because more than one person is trying to talk at the same time. *"Weird"* can be chewing gum in all meetings to stop me from rocking back and forth and struggling to understand how to look people in their eyes. It can also mean to redo the same slide over and over to fix minuscule pixel misalignments no one would ever notice, rereading emails ten times to make sure the tone feels *"normal"*, mentally rehearsing what to say at the next meeting or repeatedly preparing how I'll introduce myself at a networking event. And I don't mean casually preparing, I mean preparing every single word, the order, the tone, the facial expressions etc. And being *"weird"* can also be to take everything literally and struggling to understand nuance, jokes or sarcasm. And I still struggle with that and therefore, I require time to process. Weird can also mean feeling other people's moods in your whole body, as if the tension in the room settles in your chest or stomach and changes your breathing without you even noticing. It can also mean having a script running in your head while you speak, and still walking away replaying the conversation, convinced you said something wrong.

I remember one meeting where I shared my thoughts clearly and calmly, or so I thought I did. Once the meeting was over, a senior leader who wasn't even my manager pulled me aside and said, *"You might want to watch your tone. You came across a bit too direct, maybe even confrontational."* I was stunned to say the least as I hadn't noticed at all. I replayed the meeting over and over in my head for days. I tried to understand what I said and how I had said it and how bad it must have been to warrant such feedback. I couldn't fully grasp it, but I felt so much shame and guilt for having done something wrong without fully understanding how I had done it. Filled with shame and wanting to redeem myself, I went in full overcorrection mode and not just at the next meeting but for months. To do so, I made myself smaller in meetings, second-guessed my tone and I rehearsed ways to sound softer, lighter and more pleasant. I told myself I was being professional, but really, I was just learning how to disappear and how to be nice over being opinionated.

If you've ever felt like that, replaying a meeting in your head, wishing you could be smaller, softer, less noticeable, you're not alone. But here's the truth: your weirdness isn't the problem, it's the part of you that holds the most power.

The Invisible Work of Seeming Normal

We have been taught that leadership has a look, a tone and a posture. It should be polished and confident with a steady voice, fluent answers, and a firm handshake. Leaders are expected to sit tall, hold eye contact without breaking, smile at the right times, and use open hand gestures. They should look calm under pressure, speak without notes, and never lose their train of thought. Anything outside that mold is quickly judged. Doodling while people speak is seen as disengaged, fidgeting with a toy or a pen, bouncing your legs around or twisting a ring repeatedly for minutes on end is labeled as nervous or immature. Avoiding eye contact is considered evasive and speaking too quickly, too directly or in a monotone way is considered unpolished or lacking professionalism. But this mold is narrow and outdated as it doesn't consider that some people concentrate and work better by regulating themselves through fidgeting, doodling or moving their body.

In many organizations, leadership is still defined by sameness. There's an unspoken expectation that we should all sound the same, behave the same, think the same. And the more senior you become, the more this pressure intensifies. It's not just knowing your job and how to do it, it's also how to perform the part.

While being different is often considered a threat to leadership, because we tend to trust what feels familiar and mistake similarity for competence, being different is also a source of innovation, resilience and more often than not, relevance.

Decades of research in organizational psychology and behavioral economics show that diverse teams consistently outperform homogenous ones, not in spite of their differences but because of them[17]. What slows them down in the short term are conflicts, frictions and uncomfortable conversations, which can actually strengthen problem solving and decision-making over time.

And yet, knowing this doesn't mean we create environments where differences are truly welcomed. The problem is not the lack of different perspectives, it is how quickly those perspectives are filtered, softened or dismissed before they even land.

In the case of neurodivergent leaders, this conflict is unrelenting. We're supposed to conceal, change or recalculate our thoughts or rephrase them in a way that other people can understand easily and ensure we keep everyone comfortable. That work is hidden, yet tiresome. Some of us are left to do two jobs - the 'real' job, and the role we reinvent in an effort to fit in.

The additional effort creates distance between who we are and how we are allowed to show up. Gradually, we internalize the message that the way we process, lead, or engage is somehow less valid. This is what social theorists call epistemic injustice[18], the subtle but powerful devaluation of certain ways of knowing, speaking, and being. It happens when we are misread as distant because we avoid eye contact, incompetent because we pause to think, or abrasive because we speak plainly without softening our words.

But here's the paradox: the very filters we're asked to apply are often the ones that dull our edges. Take them away, and what remains is something incredibly valuable: unedited clarity. The work of constant self-editing may make us more palatable, but it also blunts the precision of how we think.

Many neurodivergent leaders are especially strong at spotting inconsistencies, identifying patterns, or asking the questions others overlook. That's not disruption for its own sake, it's a different cognitive wiring. In environments where groupthink and excessive politeness dominate, that difference can become an advantage.

The more you trust your way of thinking and leading, the more others will learn to trust it too. The more we give ourselves permission to lead in our own way, the more space we create for others to do the same. Being different won't always be easy, but being the same isn't a leadership strategy.

The Cost of Hiding

There is a moment many of us recognize, even if we rarely talk about it. You say something, perhaps a question or an observation that feels perfectly reasonable in your head, and for a brief second everything seems normal. Then someone laughs, or the room falls quiet, or a few people exchange a look you can't quite interpret. The shift is subtle, but unmistakable and you feel it in your body before you fully understand it in your mind. Your stomach tightens, heat rises to your face and you begin replaying what you just said, searching for the flaw. Was it obvious? Was it inappropriate? Did I misunderstand something everyone else already knew? The embarrassment is not just about being wrong, it's about suddenly feeling exposed, as if the way your mind works has been put on display.

For some, the first time this moment happened was early in life. For others, it happened in a classroom, or at work or at a networking event. The setting changes, but the lesson is the same, speaking naturally can carry a cost. And so, slowly and almost imperceptibly, we begin to adjust. We soften our tone, we rehearse before we speak, we watch how others phrase their ideas and mimic their delivery. We learn which parts of our thinking are acceptable and which parts are better edited out.

Over time, that editing becomes automatic. What started as one uncomfortable moment becomes a pattern of self correction, not because we lack insight, but because we have learned that difference draws attention.

Because of this, you actually start checking the conditions before you speak out. You edit yourself before anyone else has a chance to do it. You become a master of corporate language and small talk and you learn when to stay quiet, when to mimic, when to blend in.

And from the outside, it looks like you're doing fine.

People see you as a person who's flexible, a professional, and a good co-worker. You get appreciation for your calmness, you get praised for your composure and you get promoted for your polish. And all the while, no one sees how much this is costing you. You're doing two jobs inside: the work and the work of being the way people expect you to be.

Psychologists refer to this as *impression management*[19]. Impression management is the ongoing effort to shape how others see you. For neurodivergent people and anyone who feels different, this effort becomes a full-time job and it has a high cost. It includes emotional exhaustion, decision fatigue and a chronic sense that you're never quite doing it right.

Sociologist Arlie Hochschild introduced the concept of *emotional labor*[20] to describe the invisible effort required to manage feelings and emotional expressions in professional settings. Over time, the idea has expanded to capture other forms of hidden work as well. For many of us, that labor extends far beyond facial expressions. It includes social decoding, tone modulation, and physical self control, all performed to make others comfortable.

The problem with impression management and its emotional labor is that over time, you lose sight of what's performance and what's actually *you*. You feel foggy, you feel disconnected from your instincts, you become unsure if your silence is wisdom or just fear. You just don't know anymore. For many, this also leads to waking up tired even when you sleep well. And then you start to wonder if success is worth it if it costs you your clarity and authenticity.

In his research, psychologist Gabor Maté writes about the deep connection between *self-suppression* and *stress-related illness*[21]. When we chronically abandon our own needs, traits, or boundaries to meet external expectations, we don't just lose energy, we lose our sense of self.

In other words, it's not your weirdness or being different that drains you, it's your never ending effort to hide it, to blend in and to fit in.

Once, at a company offsite, I had to leave a breakout session because someone's perfume was so overpowering that it clouded my brain and I could not focus at all. Within minutes, I couldn't engage in the conversation and participate in what we were supposed to do. To escape, I faked having a call and slipped out, not because I didn't care but because my body simply couldn't handle it. For the next hour I sat outside, replaying it with shame, convincing myself I had failed some basic test of professionalism and that I shouldn't be so easily impacted by small things like perfumes. I wasn't broken, I was overwhelmed and I was allowed to be, but the shame of being so sensitive to smells still showed up.

Another time, during a leadership Q&A, I couldn't focus on what was being said because the chair I was sitting on was too high for me and made my feet dangle. I know it sounds silly, but sitting there with feet dangling like a 5 year old in a bus made me feel completely unanchored. Everyone else seemed completely fine even if I could see others, shorter people, also sitting there with dangling feet. I spent the entire session masking my discomfort, pretending I was engaged, even though all I wanted was a chair where my feet could touch the floor. That's when I realized that hiding how I felt wasn't only in the big moments, but it happened all the time, even in the most anecdotal ways.

When I started unmasking in small ways, saying what I actually thought, stopping the apologetic tone, letting myself be intense, something shifted. Not just in me, but also with others. Not everyone liked it and some people said they didn't recognize me and that I had changed. While some people commented trying to indicate I should go back to who I was before, other people leaned in and started to reach out. And more importantly than what people thought of me, I started to hear and feel myself again.

Because in the end, your weird has never been your weakness, it has always been your superpower.

Self-acceptance isn't passive. It's not about giving up or lowering your standards, it's about reclaiming your voice before the world filtered it out.

So, if like me, you've been filtering yourself more than you should have, hear me when I say this to you:

You weren't too much. You were misunderstood.

You weren't off. You were attuned.

You weren't broken. You were hiding.

You don't have to hide anymore.

And this is where the story shifts. Because when you stop hiding, when you slowly begin to trust the way your mind works instead of constantly correcting it, something else happens. You don't just feel lighter, you become clearer. The energy that used to go into self-editing becomes available for thinking, deciding, leading.

The directness you once softened becomes precision. The intensity you tried to mute becomes focus. The sensitivity you felt ashamed of becomes awareness of what others miss. The tendency to question what doesn't make sense becomes strategic thinking instead of disruption.

What I once called *"too much"* is now what allows me to see patterns earlier, to name tensions in the room before they escalate, to sit with complexity without rushing to easy answers. The same traits that made me feel out of place in certain meetings are the ones that now allow me to lead through ambiguity with steadiness and clarity.

That is the paradox at the heart of this rule: the parts of you that felt hardest to carry are often the parts that carry you the furthest.

Greta Thunberg didn't become powerful by adjusting herself to be more acceptable. She became powerful because she refused to dilute what made her uncomfortable to others. The urgency, the bluntness, the unwillingness to perform likability were not accidents. They were the very traits that made her credible, because they came from the way her mind works, not from an attempt to fit expectations.

Your weirdness works the same way. It's not something you overcome on your way to leadership. It's not a phase you grow out of once you become more polished. It's the foundation of how you think, how you notice, how you connect, how you challenge, and how you create.

The world doesn't need you slightly edited, it needs you fully weird.

And the moment you stop spending your energy on hiding is the moment that energy starts working for you.

Tips and Tools: Leading Without Shrinking

You don't need to minimize who you are to lead effectively. To lead, you just need to stay connected to your actual self, the one who thinks differently, notices more, feels deeper. Being different isn't a weakness but it can actually be your edge.

Here are five practices that can help you lead without shrinking and becoming someone you don't recognize.

1. Notice When You're Shape-Shifting

Start by observing your own patterns. Do you switch tone mid-sentence to sound softer? Do you rewrite Slack or Teams messages to seem "less intense"? Do you leave meetings feeling like you were playing a part and wonder if you should have been an actor?

Those moments might seem small, even harmless. But they are rarely random, they are signals. They often reveal the subtle adjustments we make to stay acceptable, to stay safe, or to stay liked.

These are the moments you suppress something real out of fear of how it will be received. It happens quickly and often automatically. For hypersensitive people, neurodivergent professionals, or anyone who has learned that fitting in feels safer than standing out, this often shows up as code switching or people pleasing. You become hyper aware of how you are being perceived and start editing yourself before anyone else has the chance to do it.

You don't need to fix this right away or change all at once. It's a process and it starts by simply noticing when it happens. And by doing so, that awareness will become a form of self-trust. Noticing your changes is the first step toward unlearning the need to shape shift, and toward trusting that the traits you edit out may be the very ones that give you clarity and edge.

Try This:
After your next meeting, write down any moments where you adjusted your tone, avoided saying something, or acted out of alignment with your instincts. And once you wrote it down, ask yourself *"what was I protecting?"* or *"why did I do it"*.

2. Practice Small Unmaskings
Unmasking doesn't have to be dramatic, especially not at work. You don't need to announce your differences, your introversion, your sensitivity, or your neurodivergence, and you don't need to stop masking overnight. You can start small.

For example, let your real facial expression show instead of faking a smile. Ask the blunt or honest question you usually keep to yourself or tone down. Let yourself stim gently if that helps you regulate yourself.

In *Unmasking Autism*, Devon Price describes unmasking as a gradual process of reclaiming parts of yourself that were hidden for survival. It isn't about dramatic exposure, it's about slowly expanding the space in which you can show up as you are.[14]

Try This:
In your next email, replace the word *"just"* or *"sorry"* with a clear, confident sentence. Notice how it feels in your body to send it without softening yourself.

Choose one meeting this week and decide in advance what one small unmasking will look like for you. Be specific. It might be asking the question you would normally soften. It might be pausing instead of filling silence. It might be keeping your neutral face instead of performing warmth.

Or, if regulation is what you usually hide, allow yourself a subtle version of it. Doodle while listening, sit in a way that feels grounded, take a sip of water before responding instead of rushing.

These are not dramatic gestures, they are small experiments. The goal is not to shock the room, it's to notice that the room doesn't collapse when you show up slightly more as yourself. And over time, those small moments of alignment remind you that what you thought you had to hide may actually be the source of your clarity and strength.

3. Impose Time to Think

Many people, including neurodivergent professionals, process information deeply, slowly, or simply differently. What looks like hesitation is often layered cognition, what looks like silence can be analysis and what looks like disengagement may actually be a second layer of thinking happening beneath the surface.

Some people think best in depth, not in speed. They need a moment to process before responding, to test an idea internally before speaking it aloud. And yet, most corporate environments prize rapid responses, polished delivery, and real time brainstorming modes that can quietly exclude reflective thinkers. Speed is often mistaken for competence and fluency is mistaken for confidence.

But depth creates clarity and clarity is a leadership asset.

Instead of apologizing for your pace, reframe it as part of your value. Let your team know that your best contributions often come after time to reflect. Normalize circling back later with your full thoughts, not just your first draft.

You can even model this explicitly. At the end of a meeting, say, *"I'd like to think this through properly and follow up with my perspective."* Over time, that becomes part of your leadership rhythm. It signals care, precision, and intentionality, not slowness.

And here is the paradox: when one person slows the tempo, others often feel relief. Not everyone thrives in spontaneous ideation and many people are silently grateful for a culture where depth is allowed.

Try This:

Before your next meeting, decide in advance that you will not rush your thinking. If a question comes your way and you are not ready, say, *"I want to give that a thoughtful answer. Let me come back to you later today."*

After the meeting, send a short follow up note with your refined thoughts. Notice how it changes the quality of your contribution and the way others respond.

You can also build structural thinking time into your leadership. You can do so by sending pre-reads before meetings, suggesting asynchronous input before decisions and creating moments where reflection is expected, not exceptional.

Imposing time to think is not a weakness, it's a way of protecting the depth that makes your perspective valuable in the first place.

4. Find Your Signal-Readers

You don't need everyone to understand you. In fact, they won't. But you do need a few people who genuinely see you and don't misinterpret your depth as distance, your silence as incompetence, or your directness as hostility.

Signal-readers are those colleagues who understand your frequency. They value substance over performance, they don't panic when you pause, they don't mistake your processing time for disengagement and they recognize the pattern in your thinking even when it isn't packaged as charisma.

Every leader needs at least one person in the room who reads their signal correctly.

When you don't have that, you start recalibrating constantly. You second-guess your tone, you overexplain and you edit yourself before you speak. But when someone in the room understands how you operate, your nervous system relaxes. You think more clearly and you lead more steadily.

This is not about creating an echo chamber. It's about creating a base and a place where your way of thinking is understood without translation. And here's something important: signal-readers are not always senior people. Sometimes they are peers and sometimes they are direct reports. What matters is not hierarchy, it's alignment.

Try This:

Identify one person at work who consistently makes you feel safe, more coherent and never smaller. Book time with them this month, not to network, but to build relational trust.

In your next high stakes meeting, notice who in the room tends to read you accurately. Position yourself near them, make eye contact with them when you speak and let their presence anchor you.

And if you don't currently have a signal-reader, that is not a personal failure. Take it instead as information. It may mean you need to be more intentional about where and with whom you invest your energy when it comes to building relationships at work.

Your weird doesn't need universal approval. It needs resonance with a few people who understand how you think, so you can feel anchored instead of constantly adjusting yourself.

5. Redefine Professionalism for Yourself

Much of what we call *"professional"* is rooted in narrow, often neurotypical, and historically white or male coded norms. Eye contact held for just the right amount of time, a firm handshake, a steady voice, effortless verbal fluency, calm composure at all times and emotional restraint.

Over time, we internalize these professional characteristics. We start believing that professionalism is about performance and about looking comfortable in rooms that were not built with us in mind. But professionalism should not be about conformity, it should be about integrity, clarity, reliability, and contribution.

When professionalism becomes assimilation, the standard is not excellence. The standard is similarity.

Redefining professionalism means asking yourself harder questions:

- What does excellence look like with my way of thinking?
- What does preparation look like with my rhythm?
- What does leadership sound like in my voice?

It may mean you prepare more deeply instead of speaking spontaneously. It may mean you lead with written clarity instead of verbal dominance. It may mean you show care through precision rather than charm.

When you redefine professionalism on your terms, you stop chasing approval and start anchoring professionalism in values.

Try This:

Take ten minutes and write your own definition of professionalism. Not the company's, not the industry's, not the one you read in leadership books, but yours.

Include the qualities that actually matter to you. For example, professionalism might mean:

- Being respectful in disagreement
- Listening fully before responding
- Asking clear and thoughtful questions
- Being prepared and doing the work
- Following through on commitments
- Communicating directly without being cruel
- Giving credit generously
- Admitting when you don't know
- Respecting other people's time and boundaries
- Staying calm without pretending you are unaffected

Notice how different this list (or your list) might feel from the traditional markers of professionalism. None of these require charisma, flawless eye contact, or perfect small talk. What this list requires is integrity.

Then ask yourself: where am I already doing this? And where am I still trying to match someone else's definition of professionalism instead of my own?

For the next week, choose one small way to embody your definition of professionalism deliberately. It might be sending clearer follow up notes, it might be setting boundaries around preparation time, it might be allowing yourself to pause without apologizing.

Professionalism is not a costume, it's a standard. The question is whose standard you are living by.

Visual Summary

Practice	**What It Looks Like**	**Why It Works**
1. Notice When You're Shape-Shifting	Catch yourself changing tone, softening opinions, hiding traits, or over-preparing to appear *"normal."*	Builds self-awareness and helps you reconnect with the traits you've been editing out, which may be your edge.
2. Practice Small Unmaskings	Use your real tone in emails. Let your natural facial expression stay. Ask the question you'd normally soften. State needs clearly.	Shows that you can be respected without performing and builds confidence in your unfiltered leadership style.
3. Impose Time to Think	Pause before answering. Say you'll follow up. Build reflection time into meetings. Stop performing speed as competence.	Protects your depth, reduces masking, and models a healthier pace for decision-making.
4. Find Your Signal-Readers	Gravitate toward colleagues who understand your frequency. Test ideas with people who value clarity over polish.	Creates psychological safety, reduces constant recalibration, and anchors your confidence in rooms that misread you.
5. Redefine Professionalism for Yourself	Define professionalism by integrity, clarity, follow-through, and respect, not polish or charisma. Question which norms you're mimicking unnecessarily.	Shifts leadership from performance to authenticity and makes space for new, more inclusive models of influence.

Micro-Practice: Say the Real Thing

Change rarely happens in dramatic moments, it happens in small repetitions. The way you speak, pause, edit or shrink yourself has been practiced for years. You don't undo that in one day based on a few insights. You undo it over time with small experiments.

Micro practices are not about reinvention, they are about recalibration. They give your nervous system proof that you can show up slightly more as yourself and survive it. And over time, those small moments build trust with yourself.

In your next conversation, say the thing you usually soften or rephrase without doing so. Don't do it to shock people but to be honest and see how the room reacts.

It might be:

- A direct question
- An idea that feels off script
- A sentence in your natural tone instead of your corporate voice

By doing so you break the habit of translating yourself. It can also help build tolerance for realness, both for you and others. It shows yourself and others what's possible when truth replaces performance.

Try it once, feel how it goes and when you're ready, try it again. Over time, you'll stop rehearsing and start leading from your core and from the real you.

Practical Quick Phrases

One of the hardest parts of embracing our differences is finding the right words to make it an asset in the moment. In such a situation, most of the time, people either opt to keep silent or to excessively explain themselves. Preparing several phrases beforehand can help you in presenting your viewpoint without feeling obligated to prove your point. Personally, I use these kinds of anchor points as a way to signal confidence, share ideas that may sound unconventional, and remind both myself and others that being different brings something important to the table. Here are some examples of quick phrases I use:

- I see it differently, let me share why.
- I tend to notice patterns or details others might miss.
- My strength isn't speed, it's depth.
- Here's an angle we have not considered yet.

- I need a moment to process before I respond. I'll come back with a clearer answer.
- I work best when I can go deep on this instead of spreading across too many things.
- I work best when I can bring my full perspective, even if it's different.

Checklist: What Will You Try This Week?

Before you move on, choose one or two of these to experiment with this coming week. Don't try to do them all, only one of two to help you interrupt the habit of shrinking.

- Notice when you shift your tone, words, or posture to fit in.
- Practice a moment of unmasking this week.
- Give yourself permission to process at your own pace.
- Allow yourself to speak in your natural tone, even if it feels risky.
- Spend time with people who value your way of thinking.
- Reflect on what leadership looks like for you and act accordingly.
- Say "no" or "I don't know" without apologizing.

Closing: The Power of Leading Without Editing Yourself

I can be very blunt, and I used to think my directness was a flaw. I also believed that my sensitivity was something I had to manage quietly, something to compensate for. So I softened, I filtered, I studied other people who seemed more relaxed, more polished, more charming, and I tried to follow their lead.

But I never felt at home in their version of leadership and that's because it wasn't mine. It took me years to understand that my differences weren't something to hide, but instead something I should be building from.

Organizational psychologist Adam Grant has written about how non-conformity is often a marker of originality, and that many of the most successful change-makers were once seen as outliers. Not because they fit the mold, but because they didn't.[22] They kept showing up in ways that didn't match expectations, and over time, that difference became their strength.

Psychologist Brené Brown distinguishes between fitting in and belonging. Fitting in, she argues, requires us to assess a situation and become who we need to be in order to be accepted, whereas belonging requires us to show up as we are.[23] And leadership, real leadership, is far closer to belonging than to fitting in.

And for many neurodivergent professionals, introverts, overthinkers, highly sensitive people and original minds, the cost of fitting in isn't just emotional. It's also mentally and physically exhausting. The exhaustion of masking, of constantly translating ourselves into something more palatable, has a name. Psychologist Devon Price calls it camouflage cost.[14] It's the wear and tear of never feeling safe enough to lead as we really are.

Leadership isn't about blending in, it's about becoming more ourselves, on purpose.

If you don't fit the mold, remember this: you're not too intense, too direct, or too sensitive. You're not too much. What you are is unfiltered. And in environments that reward polish and performance, that can feel risky.

But risk is also where trust begins. Not the kind built on charm or likability, but the kind built on consistency and clarity. When people know what they're getting from you, when your tone matches your thinking, when your values match your voice, something steadier emerges. That steadiness builds credibility.

People may label you as intense, awkward, or even weird. Let them. Their words don't diminish your value. If anything, they often reveal how uncomfortable people are with differences they don't control.

You don't need to seem normal. You need to be real. Because the parts of you that once felt inconvenient are often the very traits that make you perceptive, precise, and brave.

And that's how you lead.
Anyway.

Rule 3: You Feel Like an Impostor

"Doubt kills more dreams than failure ever will."
Suzy Kassem

I used to think leadership came with a feeling, a feeling of certainty, readiness and of legitimacy. I imagined I'd wake up one day and I'd just know I was ready, but that feeling never came.

A few years ago, a woman I mentor, Marie, was promoted to Director. She called me the morning after the announcement. *"I thought I'd feel different,"* she said. *"More certain, more... legitimate."* She had assumed something would shift inside her overnight, that the title would settle into her body and quiet the voice that had followed her for years. She expected to wake up feeling ready without a trace of doubt, as if the promotion itself would confirm not only that she deserved it, but also finally allow her to believe in herself. After all, she had spent years working toward this moment, outperforming expectations, preparing thoroughly, thinking deeply, and still privately wondering whether others saw through her, whether they sensed the effort it took to appear as composed as she did. That morning, standing in her kitchen holding her coffee, she found herself waiting for the feeling of readiness to arrive. It didn't come. Instead, she felt the opposite. The doubts were louder, not quieter, and she caught herself wondering whether this had all been a mistake.

Later that same day, she walked into her first leadership team meeting in her new role feeling like an outsider who had somehow slipped into a room that required a different version of her. She didn't feel as though she had earned her stripes to be there and felt slightly fraudulent pretending to belong. The others around her appeared more decisive, more articulate, more certain in their tone and in their presence. She spent part of the meeting listening carefully and the other part mentally drafting what she might say if she were asked to contribute, replaying and refining her thoughts before they were even spoken. The familiar internal monologue surfaced again: *Do I really belong here? Am I actually ready for this level of responsibility?*

At one point, someone raised a challenge she had seen coming months earlier and had already spent time thinking through. She had quietly mapped possible solutions, considered implications, and anticipated objections long before the meeting took place. When the room went quiet and no one spoke, she cleared her throat and offered her perspective, carefully but clearly. Her point landed and heads nodded. One of the other leaders asked her to elaborate further. In that moment, nothing dramatic happened and her doubt didn't vanish, but something else shifted. She realized that she didn't have to feel ready to add value. She didn't have to feel completely legitimate in order to contribute meaningfully. She still wasn't entirely sure she belonged, but she spoke anyway. She didn't feel ready, but she led anyway.

When Jacinda Ardern was elected Prime Minister of New Zealand at the age of 37, she revealed that she sometimes felt like she didn't have enough experience to be in her position. After the shootings at the mosque in Christchurch, she managed the transition from grief to change in the country, not with a show of strength but with deep empathy and uncertainty which she showed without hiding. In interviews and public reflections, Ardern has acknowledged the uncertainty that accompanies leadership. She has spoken about how, even at the highest level of responsibility, she would pause and ask herself whether she was making the right decisions and doing right by the people she served. But she didn't let that self-questioning stop her from showing up with clarity and compassion. She didn't always feel ready, but she led anyway.[24]

And maybe you feel like Marie or Jacinda Ardern. Maybe you don't feel ready or confident enough to take the lead. And for that reason or because you fear feeling like an impostor, you have not dared step forward, you have not tried to become a leader or call yourself that.

We often imagine leadership as a destination. We imagine it's a place we go to, a point where the self-doubt quiets down and certainty settles in. A place you attain where you know what's best and how to manage leading others. It sounds great, but such a destination doesn't exist for most of us. Research in developmental psychology tells that story. According to Dr. Jennifer Garvey Berger, leadership development isn't about arriving at a fixed identity, it's about growing our capacity to navigate complexity and act with intention in uncertain situations.[25]

And that capacity to navigate complexity and act with intention in uncertain situations isn't born out of confidence but it's built through discomfort and repeated experiences.

But because of this misconception that leadership is a destination, most of us wait to feel ready before we act. Not just when it comes to leading others but for so many facets of life. We wait to feel confident before we speak or we wait for someone else to validate us before we step forward. We wait to get proof that we're ready to take the leap. We wait until we acquire all the expertise we believe is needed and we wait until all pieces fall into place. But sadly, that moment rarely comes on its own. And it potentially comes even less often if you're neurodivergent, introverted, sensitive, or simply someone who doesn't match the dominant prototype of leadership. If you're any of these archetypes, you actually might wait forever because the systems around you weren't designed to reflect your strength back to you and make you feel like you're ready to leap forward. And because the system wasn't designed for you, you might feel like an impostor, even when you're fully capable.

Here is the hard truth: waiting to feel ready keeps you stuck in the loop of doubt. Readiness doesn't arrive before the leap, it's actually built by taking it.

And that's why this rule exists: *You Feel Like an Impostor*. Not to convince you that you're fearless or invincible, but to remind you that fear isn't the enemy of leadership and that hesitation doesn't disqualify you. Let's be honest, the presence of doubt doesn't negate your ability to make decisions or your ability to guide others or to be an agent of change.

The question isn't whether you feel ready, but the question is whether you're willing to move anyway, even if you hesitate, even if you're scared and even if the voice in your head is still whispering, *"Are you sure?"*

You don't need to be sure. What you need is to begin and to lead anyway.

Waiting Won't Make You a Leader

We're taught to think leadership begins when we feel confident and when we feel ready. And that myth isn't just driven by personal doubt, it's driven by corporate cultures and systems. And that's because too often organizations reward the appearance of certainty, even when it's shallow, and organizations dismiss quieter forms of leadership, even when they're thoughtful. I know I'm generalizing, but such rewards have been in place for decades and although there are exceptions, those are usually the norm.

Most leaders, especially those who don't fit the traditional mold, carry a quiet belief that they're not quite ready or that they're not yet qualified enough or that they're not extroverted enough or that they're not strategic enough. This belief doesn't mean they're unfit to lead, it means they're paying attention to how organizations operate and who's being promoted to leadership positions around them. As most people being promoted don't resemble them, they believe they're not leadership material or that more professional growth is required on their part.

The experience many of us now refer to as *"impostor syndrome"* was first described in 1978 by psychologists Pauline Clance and Suzanne Imes, who called it the *"impostor phenomenon."*[26]. They used that term intentionally, describing a pattern among high achieving individuals who persistently believed their success was undeserved and feared being exposed as frauds, despite clear evidence of competence. Over time, the label "impostor syndrome" entered popular culture, even though the original researchers did not frame it as a clinical disorder. Since then, research has shown that these feelings are far from rare. A 2020 systematic review found that a majority of professionals report experiencing impostor thoughts at some point in their lives, with some estimates suggesting that up to 70 percent encounter it at least once.[27] It appears especially common among high performers and among those navigating environments where they feel underrepresented, including women, people of color, and neurodivergent individuals. The irony is that the very people who question their legitimacy the most are often the ones who care the most deeply about doing their work well.

After years of hiding parts of ourselves (as explored in Rule 2), it's easy to believe we need to *"fix"* our doubts before we can lead. And by fixing, we mean to eliminate the doubts. But what if doubt wasn't the problem but instead it was just part of the path?

I spent my whole career in doubt of my own capabilities, but I was already a Vice President in a large multinational company employing thousands of people when the doubts hit hardest. From the outside, it all looked impressive: the job title, the team, the meetings, the strategy decks, but inside, I often felt like I was one question away from being identified as a fraud or for everyone to realize I didn't belong. I felt as if, at any point in time, I could say something that would make everyone realize I didn't know what I was doing and that I didn't have the credentials to do my job. I feared people would realize I wasn't ready to be this Vice President I had become. And not because I lacked the experience or because I didn't work hard, but because the version of leadership I saw around me never felt like it included someone like me.

I wasn't loud, I didn't dominate conversations, I felt easily intimidated by loud senior leaders (I still do) and I didn't speak just to be heard or to take room. I listened quietly often, especially in high level meetings where I felt everyone was more clever than I was, I observed, I took time to process and sometimes that made me feel like I was falling behind even when the work I delivered was sound or my team was thriving.

I remember often thinking, *"What if today is the day someone realizes I don't actually know what I'm doing?"* And I thought this more times than I care to admit. But even though I felt that way and still do sometimes, I kept showing up. And over time and very *slowly* I must admit, I learned that I didn't need to feel ready to lead. I just needed to be present. I didn't need to know all the answers, I needed to ask good questions. I didn't need to perform with confidence, I needed to model clarity and consistency.

I still have days when the impostor voice shows up. I still overthink how I speak, how I'm perceived, my decisions, what will happen tomorrow and if I'm good enough. I still have moments when I wonder if I'm too different to belong in the corporate world and if I should instead find a completely different new career.

But regardless of those moments and doubts, I lead anyway. And I do so because that voice of doubt and insecurity doesn't get to decide what I'm capable of. I do, or at least I try to convince myself that I do.

The traditional narrative around leadership promotes certainty and decisiveness as default traits. But studies in adaptive leadership, particularly the work of Ronald Heifetz and colleagues, suggest that leadership in complex environments is less about providing definitive answers and more about mobilizing people to face difficult realities while tolerating uncertainty.[28] That kind of leadership doesn't require confidence first, it requires resilience and courage.

And courage isn't the absence of fear, to the contrary, it's acting with purpose in the presence of fear. Psychologist Brené Brown has written extensively about the relationship between vulnerability and courage.[29] She argues that vulnerability is not weakness but uncertainty, risk, and emotional exposure, and that courage is impossible without it. In other words, you cannot be brave without stepping into situations where you are unsure. Reading her work helped me realize that what I had labelled as hesitation or self-doubt was often something else entirely, it was the emotional exposure that comes with caring deeply about the outcome. And that, in itself, is a form of courage.

If leadership inevitably involves moments of self-questioning, then for those of us who are used to doubting ourselves, this realization is both unsettling and freeing. It is unsettling because it means clarity may never fully arrive before action is required. We may not get the clean internal signal that tells us we are finally ready. But it is also freeing, because it suggests that feeling unsure is not evidence that something is wrong with us. It's not proof that we're unqualified or out of place. It's simply part of being humans in positions of responsibility.

The truth is that leadership is not something you grow into once the fear disappears, it's something you practice while the fear is still present. It's built through action, through contribution, through speaking even when your voice feels slightly unsteady. Confidence rarely precedes the act. Instead, more often than not, it follows it.

So if you are still waiting for the moment when you finally feel like a *"real leader,"* consider the possibility that the feeling may not arrive first. Leadership is not a state you enter once doubt is gone, it's a choice you make in spite of it. And sometimes, the most honest form of leadership is simply deciding to move forward anyway.

When Self-Doubt and Leadership Coexist

For years, I held onto a secret I thought would discredit me as a leader: I often had no idea what I was doing (I still often have no idea to be honest).

In August 2023, I wrote a blog post with that exact title *"Corporate Life: I Don't Always Know What I'm Doing."* [30] And in a moment of courage, I shared my post not just on my website but on LinkedIn in hope it would help liberate me from the fear of being discredited. I wrote the blog after a day full of back-to-back meetings, strategic decisions, last-minute presentations, and being the person people turn to for answers. I remember closing my laptop and thinking, *"How am I the one leading all this?"* Not out of false modesty, but out of genuine bewilderment that I was seen as the expert, when inside, I still felt like I was figuring it out in real time. The best comparison I have is to compare this to adulthood itself. Most of us move through life quietly wondering when we will finally feel like *"real"* adults, when we will become what adults seemed to be when we were children. Being a leader feels similar to me. It's this constant questioning and quiet realization that I may never fully feel like a leader, just as I may never fully feel like an adult.

When I shared that post, the response surprised me. Not because the piece was particularly profound, it wasn't, but because of how many people wrote back to say they felt the same. Senior leaders, managers, early career professionals, people across industries and countries. It resonated not because it offered answers, but because it named something we rarely admit. How often do Vice Presidents or senior leaders say out loud that they don't always know what they are doing? We watch leaders navigate crises and make decisions and, in the absence of any visible doubt, we assume they must be certain. But certainty is often a performance and the internal questioning doesn't disappear just because the title changes.

And as it turns out, a lot of people feel this way. A lot of people don't know what they're doing and try their best to figure it out. And this is especially the case for those of us who were never told we were destined for leadership. Those of us who didn't see ourselves reflected in the models we were given and those of us who learned to lead by building the road as we walked it.

Dr. Valerie Young, who has written extensively about impostor syndrome, explains that many high-achieving people attribute their successes to luck, timing, or external factors, while interpreting ordinary challenges as evidence that they are frauds.[31] This dynamic can feel even more intense for people from underrepresented backgrounds. When you do not look or sound like the people historically associated with leadership, self-doubt doesn't always feel irrational, it can feel like a logical response to the signals around you.

The philosopher Miranda Fricker introduced the term epistemic injustice to describe what happens when some people are granted less credibility than others because of bias, even when what they are saying is sound.[18] In corporate settings, that bias is rarely explicit, it often shows up as "style feedback" that quietly questions your competence, your intent, or your authority, for example:

"You seem disengaged." (when you're pausing to process)
"You come across as cold." (when you're being calm or when you don't smile enough)
"You need to watch your tone." (when you're being direct)
"You might want to soften that." (when you're being clear and concise)

Individually, these comments can seem small or even reasonable. But over time, they accumulate and they shape how you see yourself and how much space you feel entitled to take.

These patterns of self-doubt don't just live inside our heads, they are reinforced by the systems around us. When organizations equate leadership with extroversion or constant visibility, people who lead differently are nudged into questioning themselves. When calmness is coded as *"cold"* or directness as *"unpolished,"* it's not merely a personal insecurity being triggered, it is a structural signal about whose style is considered legitimate and whose is not.

That is why courage, not confidence, becomes the essential leadership skill. Confidence fluctuates, courage allows you to act even when the system quietly questions your credibility.

Dr. Brené Brown describes vulnerability as *"showing up and being seen,"* and argues that it is the most accurate measure of courage.[29] Courage, in that sense, is not the absence of doubt, it's the willingness to move through uncertainty with integrity.

I've led while second-guessing myself, I've spoken up while unsure how my words would land and I've made decisions while knowing they might not be perfect and fearing they might even be wrong.

And each time, including now, I remind myself that uncertainty does not cancel out strength. I can feel unsure and still build trust, I can ask questions and still hold authority and I can acknowledge my doubts and still make decisions.

This, for me, is what leading anyway means. It means not waiting for fear to disappear or for qualification to feel complete. It means stepping forward while doubt is still present because the truth is, no one feels ready all the time and yet, we lead anyway.

Tips and Tools: How to Lead While Feeling Like an Impostor

1. Name the Doubt.

Impostor thoughts thrive in silence, which is why naming them matters. The moment you say, *"I'm feeling unsure right now,"* you begin to separate the doubt from your identity. And by doing so, you reduce its power. When you acknowledge the doubt, even quietly to yourself, you strip away some of the shame attached to it. And when you dare to voice it appropriately to others, you often discover that what felt like an individual weakness is a shared human experience. That shift can transform isolation into connection and vulnerability into strength.

Psychologist Dr. Kristin Neff, who pioneered research on self-compassion, explains that simply acknowledging and naming our inner experience is a critical step in reducing self-criticism. Rather than suppressing or over identifying with difficult thoughts, we learn to observe them with awareness.[32]

Try this:
Instead of asking yourself *"Why am I like this?"*, ask *"What am I feeling?"* and *"What do I need?"* These small shifts move you from self-judgment to recognition and from shame to self-compassion.

And remember that acknowledging your doubts doesn't make you weak, it makes you honest and that is where trust starts.

2. Do the Work Anyway.
Confidence is not a prerequisite for leadership, but it's often the byproduct of it. The same is true for courage. You don't build courage by waiting until you feel ready, you build courage by acting while uncertainty is still present.

Psychologist Dr. Amy Cuddy, in her work on presence and embodied confidence, suggests that how we show up physically and behaviorally can influence how we experience ourselves internally.[4] Acting as if we belong, even before we fully feel it, can gradually reshape our internal narrative. This is not about pretending or performing a version of leadership that is not yours, it's about practicing into your role rather than waiting to feel perfectly aligned with it.

Every time you contribute despite your doubts, you collect evidence that you are capable. Every time you speak even though your voice feels slightly unsteady, you teach your nervous system that visibility is survivable. Over time, those small acts accumulate. What once felt threatening begins to feel manageable, what once felt like exposure begins to feel like responsibility and what once felt like risk begins to feel like growth.

Try this:
The next time you notice yourself hesitating because you're not fully certain, pause and ask yourself, *"If I had to decide right now, what would I choose?"* and then choose it. Or if a conversation stalls because no one wants to take ownership, say, *"Here's how I see it,"* and offer your perspective without over qualifying it.

You do not need to eliminate every doubt before acting, you need to tolerate having some doubt while acting. If the decision turns out imperfect, adjust. Leadership is rarely about flawless execution, it's about responsible movement.

Action does not remove fear, but it changes your relationship to it. And over time, that shift builds something deeper than confidence, it builds trust in your own capacity to lead, even when you feel unsure.

3. Track Evidence, Not Emotions.

When doubt takes over, it feels urgent and convincing. But emotions fluctuate, self-doubt spikes and settles. On the other hand, evidence tells a more stable story.

Instead of tracking how you feel, track what you do and what happens as a result.

Keep a simple *"I Did Good"* note on your phone or in a notebook. Save screenshots of positive feedback, write down successful outcomes, record moments when you spoke up, made a decision, or handled something well. On hard days, return to that evidence and let it remind you of what is objectively true.

And take this habit one step further: don't only look at your evidence log when you feel insecure, review it regularly, even on good days. Train your brain to register competence as normal rather than exceptional. Over time, you begin to internalize proof of your capability in the same way you once internalized doubt.

Psychologist Dr. Martin Seligman, founder of positive psychology, has emphasized the value of deliberately noting what goes well and why as a way to counter the brain's negativity bias.[33]

You don't have to believe in yourself all the time, but you should have evidence available when your feelings tell a different story. When doubt gets loud, let the facts speak.

4. Redefine Leadership on Your Terms.

Impostor feelings often arise when we measure ourselves against a definition of leadership that was never built with us in mind. If leadership is defined as certainty, dominance, speed, and constant visibility, then anyone who leads through reflection, deliberation, or quiet influence will inevitably feel behind.

But what if the definition itself is too narrow?

Leadership researcher Frances Frei argues that effective leadership is grounded in trust, and trust is built through authenticity, logic, and empathy.[12] It's not about projecting invulnerability or performing certainty, it's about being consistent, clear, and committed to helping others succeed.

That kind of leadership doesn't require you to become louder, it requires you to become more intentional.

When you redefine leadership on your own terms, doubt begins to shift. Instead of asking, *"Why am I not like them?"* you begin asking, *"What kind of leader am I trying to be?"* Instead of measuring yourself against charisma or dominance, you measure yourself against clarity, integrity, and impact.

Try this:
Write down three qualities that define leadership for you. Not the qualities you think organizations reward, but the qualities you genuinely respect in others. Then ask yourself where you are already embodying those traits. You may find that you are closer to leadership than you allow yourself to believe.

Redefining leadership doesn't eliminate doubt entirely, but it changes the standard you're comparing yourself against. You can be direct without being harsh, you can be quiet without being passive, you can lead with clarity without raising your voice and when the definition expands, your legitimacy often expands with it.

5. Speak Up Before You Feel Ready.

Waiting for certainty is a subtle trap. We tell ourselves we will contribute once we have thought it through one more time, once we feel fully confident in our position, once the doubt has quieted. But that moment of total internal clarity rarely arrives in the way we imagine.

Instead, we need to realize that it's possible to speak while feeling unsure and it's possible to lead while feeling slightly shaky. The presence of doubt doesn't invalidate the value of your perspective.

Organizational psychologist Adam Grant has written about how many original thinkers don't wait until they feel fully prepared before they act.[22] They often experience doubt and even procrastination, yet they move forward anyway, not because they are reckless, but because they understand that clarity is often built through engagement. Learning happens in motion, not in isolation.

When you withhold your voice until you feel completely certain, you deprive yourself of the very experiences that would build that certainty. Speaking up is not a performance of perfection, it's participation in the process.

Try this:

The next time you feel the impulse to hold back because your idea is not yet perfectly formed, share it in progress. Say, *"This is still a thought in development, but here's how I'm seeing it."* Allow yourself to contribute without polishing every edge.

Or, if you are responsible for a decision and find yourself waiting for one more piece of reassurance, set a reasonable threshold. Ask yourself, *"Do I have enough information to move responsibly?"* If the answer is yes, decide.

You do not need to feel fearless to act, you need to be willing to be visible before you feel fully comfortable. Bravery is not the disappearance of fear, it's showing up while fear is still present.

Visual Summary

Practice	What It Looks Like	Why It Works
1. Name the Doubt	Say out loud: *"I'm feeling unsure right now."*	Reduces shame and normalizes self-doubt. Creates psychological distance from impostor thoughts.
2. Do the Work Anyway	Act even if you feel uncertain. Speak up. Make the decision.	Builds courage through action. Teaches your nervous system that uncertainty is survivable.
3. Track Evidence, Not Emotions	Keep an *"I Did Good"* note with proof of feedback, outcomes, and contributions. Review it regularly.	Counters negativity bias. Replaces emotional distortion with objective evidence.
4. Redefine Leadership on Your Terms	Write down three leadership qualities you genuinely respect and identify where you already embody them.	Expands your definition of legitimacy. Shifts comparison from performance to values.
5. Speak Up Before You Feel Ready	Share your idea in progress or decide once you have enough information.	Builds confidence through participation. Creates clarity through engagement.

Micro-Practice: Separate the Voice from the Facts

This practice trains you to distinguish between doubt and reality.

The next time you notice impostor thoughts rising, pause and write down two columns:

Column 1: *What the doubt is saying.*
For example:
"I don't belong here."
"I'm not experienced enough."
"They're going to realize I'm not qualified."

Column 2: *The observable facts.*
For example:
"I was hired for this role."
"I prepared for this meeting."
"I have delivered results before."

Do not argue with the doubt, just separate it from the evidence. The goal is not to silence the voice, it's to prevent it from becoming your only source of truth.

Over time, this simple act of separation builds cognitive steadiness. You learn that doubt can speak, but it does not get to decide.

Practical Quick Phrases

When impostor thoughts show up, many of us instinctively retreat. We over prepare, overthink, or default to silence because we believe leadership requires certainty. But in reality, carefully voiced uncertainty can build more trust than performative confidence.

The goal is not to confess incompetence, it's to model thoughtful leadership. When you acknowledge limits without collapsing into self-doubt, you signal psychological safety, intellectual honesty, and collective responsibility. You demonstrate that leadership is not about having every answer, but about staying engaged in the process.

These phrases can help you remain visible without pretending to be certain. They allow you to lead through doubt rather than hide behind it.

- *"This is new for me, so I might need your input as we go."*
- *"I don't have all the answers, but I'm confident we'll find them together."*
- *"Let's experiment, we'll learn as we go."*
- *"That's a good question. I'll think about it and come back to you."*
- *"I'm still figuring this out, but here's what I'm thinking so far."*

Used intentionally, statements like these don't diminish authority, they can recalibrate it. They replace rigid certainty with grounded presence. And over time, they teach both you and your team that leadership can coexist with learning.

Checklist: What Will You Try This Week?

You don't eliminate impostor thoughts in one breakthrough moment. You reduce their influence through repeated practice. This week, choose one or two of the actions below and experiment with leading while doubt is still present.

- Acknowledge an impostor thought out loud or in writing
- Take an action despite self-doubt
- Record one recent success to revisit when doubt returns
- Share an idea or opinion before you feel 100 percent certain
- Show up with presence even when you feel unsure

Closing: You're Not an Impostor

I used to think leadership would one day click. That, like a puzzle, the last piece would fall into place and I would finally feel ready. I believed I would cross some invisible finish line and arrive on the other side: certain of myself, fluent in the language of confidence, immune to the swirl of doubt.

As you and I both know, that day never came. What came instead was a different realization. I could spend years waiting to feel ready and never reach that state, or I could begin exactly as I was and learn as I went.

I once sat in my car outside the office, dreading a strategy meeting where I had to present. The PowerPoint was strong, the ideas were clear, but all I could think was, *"Who am I to be in that room trying to convince these people I know the way?"* I was stressed, deeply stressed, and all I wanted to do was skip the meeting, call in sick, and hide. But I knew I would regret retreating more than I would regret trying, so I went in anyway. I delivered the pitch. Not flawlessly, but clearly and honestly and with enough presence to be taken seriously. No one saw the storm inside me, all they saw was someone who had prepared, someone who was somewhat steady and someone leading. In that moment, I understood that what often looks like confidence from the outside is simply invisible courage.

Research supports this gap between how we feel and how we function. Impostor feelings disproportionately affect high performers, especially those who are conscientious or perfectionistic by nature.[27] The very people most qualified to lead are often the least likely to internalize their competence.

And the leadership models many of us were taught don't help. They favor visible certainty and charisma, even though adaptive leadership theory reminds us that leading in complex systems is not about having all the answers, but about helping people make progress through uncertainty.[34] That kind of leadership is uncomfortable. It requires emotional steadiness more than bravado. As Brené Brown teaches, courage is not the absence of fear, but the willingness to act while feeling vulnerable.[29]

Again and again, in conversations with leaders across disciplines and sectors, I've seen the same pattern. Those who feel like impostors are often the ones who care most deeply about doing the right thing. Their hesitation doesn't signal incompetence, it signals responsibility.

Psychologist Susan David describes emotional agility as the ability to experience discomfort without being controlled by it.[35] That capacity, to feel doubt without being hijacked by it, is not a weakness, it's a leadership skill.

If you are still waiting for the day when fear disappears, it may never come. Doubt doesn't vanish with a promotion, an achievement, or experience, it simply evolves.

You don't need to eliminate doubt before you lead.
You don't need to be invulnerable to be credible.
You don't need to perform certainty to earn trust.

Leadership is not the absence of fear, it's the decision to move forward while fear is still present. And sometimes, that decision is enough.

Conclusion to Part 1: Who We Are

Most leadership books begin with strategies. This one did not, it began with identity.

It began there because, for those of us who lead differently, more quietly, more slowly, or from the margins, the greatest obstacle is rarely a lack of knowledge or skill. It's the constant negotiation between who we are and who we think we are supposed to be. Every meeting, every performance review, every networking event can feel like a subtle test of whether our natural way of leading is enough.

For many of us, the doubt is not about competence, it's about legitimacy. And until we face that tension directly, no strategy or skill building will resolve the deeper insecurity.

That is why these first three rules did not offer grand tactics or ask you to become someone else. They asked you to stop hiding.

Rule 1 gave us permission to show up without performing and to lead without pretending to be more charismatic or extraverted than we actually are. It told us that presence doesn't require us to always be performing and that being confident is a skill we can build. It also reminded us that confidence isn't a prerequisite for trust. Leadership grounded in clarity and self-awareness fosters stronger engagement and resilience than leadership styles built on performance, loudness, or constant visibility.

Rule 2 moved us toward acceptance of the parts of ourselves we were taught to soften, change or even hide. It discussed how our *"weird"* doesn't have to be something we're ashamed of but it can actually be a source of wisdom. This can be especially true for introverts, highly sensitive people and neurodivergent leaders. And for anyone whose ways of thinking and interacting with other people are 'different' and break the mold. Diversity of thought improves problem solving, creativity and long-term performance, not in spite of the friction it brings, but because of it.

And Rule 3 reminded us that feeling like an impostor isn't a show stopper nor a limit that prevents us from taking the lead. It invited us to practice self-trust, kindness towards ourselves and to stop waiting for the fear to disappear before we act. This rule also reminded us that doubt doesn't disqualify us and that courage isn't about being certain, but about moving forward anyway and facing our fears. Resilience is built in discomfort and as we build our ability to be brave, we also build our confidence. And it's important to remember that those who feel like impostors are often the ones paying the most attention and they're often the ones who care the most. As Brené Brown argues, courage requires acting in alignment with your values despite fear.[29] As Ronald Heifetz's adaptive leadership theory reminds us, the best leaders aren't the ones with all the answers, they're the ones who stay present in ambiguity and move others forward.[28]

Overall, these 3 rules touch upon related themes that span across self-permission, self-acceptance and self-trust. These rules aren't about tactics but about permissions:

- Permission to lead without performing.
- Permission to bring your full self into the room.
- Permission to lead before you feel ready.

And all of this simply because your leadership doesn't begin when you finally fit the mold, it begins the moment you stop waiting to fit.

Lead anyway.

PART 2 – HOW WE LEAD

"What we do is more important than what we say or what we say we believe."
bell hooks

Not all of us were raised to see ourselves as leaders or encouraged to step forward when leadership roles appeared, in classrooms, on sports teams, or in the small moments where confidence is first rehearsed. Some of us learned to work twice as hard just to be noticed, and some of us preferred not to be noticed at all. Not everyone feels safe being visible. Many of us internalized the idea that leadership looked a certain way: loud, extroverted, always certain, always commanding. And when we didn't match that image, we concluded that leadership simply wasn't for us.

Part 1 of this book was about dismantling that idea. It was about unlearning the myth that you need charisma, confidence, or certainty to lead. Part 1 of this book was about giving yourself permission to begin, even while doubting, even while being different, even while being unsure.

Part 2 is about what comes next once you give yourself permission to lead. Permission is the beginning, not the method. So what does leadership actually look like in practice when you don't match the traditional template?

How do you lead without burning out?
How do you ask better questions in rooms that reward quick answers?
How do you build trust when you speak less but think deeply?
How do you hold space for others while protecting your own energy?
How do you lead while you are still unmasking, still healing, still figuring things out?

These are not theoretical questions, they are daily realities for anyone leading from the margins. They arise in performance reviews, in strategy meetings, in difficult conversations, and in moments when you feel the quiet pressure to perform a version of leadership that doesn't feel like yours.

This section is about practicing leadership differently. It's about setting boundaries as a cultural signal, not a personal weakness. It's about choosing curiosity over control. It's about leading with steadiness instead of spectacle. And it's about recognizing that authenticity is not a branding exercise, it is a sustainability strategy.

You will not find rigid formulas here, leadership is too human for that. What you will find are principles, tools, and lived examples that help you translate identity into action and ways to lead without erasing yourself in the process.

Leadership from the margins is not secondary leadership. It's not a diluted version of the *"real"* thing, it's necessary leadership. As our systems grow more complex and more fragile, the ability to lead with reflection, restraint, and emotional intelligence is not optional, it's foundational.

Permission was the first step.
Practice is what comes next.

Rule 4: Ask Better Questions

"Judge a person by their questions rather than by their answers."
Voltaire

When I was promoted to be a manager for the first time, I panicked.

Not because I had not worked for it, I had. I had taken on extra projects, delivered results, worked late, prepared thoroughly, and said yes to opportunities that stretched me. I had taken on tasks, assignments and roles that were way out of my comfort zone for over 4 years at that point. I wanted to become a manager, but the moment it became real, the weight of it hit me.

Of course, I didn't show the panic I felt. Instead, I proactively tried to show competence, to show readiness and to show a version of myself I believed leadership required. I did not dare say I felt unsure and overwhelmed. I didn't want to suggest, even indirectly, that promoting me might have been a mistake. I had spent too many years working to be taken seriously to risk looking unprepared.

So I became a people manager, responsible for a small team, and I was convinced I needed to have all the answers. I prepared obsessively for every meeting, I overthought scenarios before they happened, I tried to anticipate every question and every possible challenge, determined that no one would see how uncertain I sometimes felt inside.

At the time, I truly believed leadership meant having the map and showing others the way.

One afternoon, after a particularly messy team meeting where I had tried to compensate for my uncertainty by pretending I knew more than I did, I called my coach. I needed to vent. I told her I felt like a fraud, that I did not know what I was doing and that I was supposed to lead, yet I had no clear direction. I was convinced my team could sense my confusion and I feared I was losing their trust and my credibility at the same time.

She listened quietly and then she said: *"You're not supposed to have all the answers. No one ever does. You're here to ask the questions that will help the team find the answers."*

At first, I resisted because her words felt destabilizing. If I was not supposed to have the answers, then what exactly was my role? Asking questions sounded passive, it sounded like losing control. More than that, it felt like admitting I lacked the competence and certainty I believed leadership required. I had worked too hard to be seen as capable to now risk appearing unsure.

For a while, nothing changed. I kept preparing obsessively, I kept rehearsing meetings in advance and I kept walking into rooms determined to prove I belonged there.

But her words lingered.

They surfaced in meetings when I felt the familiar pressure to speak first, they echoed when someone on my team looked at me, waiting for direction. Slowly, I began experimenting, almost reluctantly. Instead of answering immediately, I paused. Instead of presenting my solution, I asked, *"What do you think we should prioritize?"* Instead of closing the discussion, I asked, *"What are we not seeing here?"*

At first, it felt uncomfortable. The silence after a question felt long and I worried the team would interpret my curiosity as hesitation. I also worried I was exposing my lack of certainty. But something unexpected happened. The conversations deepened, my team started thinking out loud, they started to challenge each other and they started to build on each other's ideas. The pressure I had felt to carry the room alone began to loosen.

It didn't happen overnight, it was a very gradual shift and it became a conscious practice. I did it one meeting at a time and slowly I stopped trying to prove I was the smartest person in the room and started trying to make the room smarter.

I started asking questions like:
"What's blocking us?"
"What problem are we actually trying to solve?"
"What assumptions are we making?"
"Whose perspective is missing?"
"What do you need from me?"
"What would success really look like?"

And something shifted.

My team began opening up in ways they never had before. They debated ideas more openly, they took ownership and they challenged each other respectfully. Insights surfaced that I could never have reached alone. Instead of waiting for direction, they started generating solutions. Instead of relying on me to define the path, they began shaping it together.

That was the moment I understood that leadership is not about showing the path forward to the team, it's about clearing the fog so others can see it for themselves.

Research supports this shift.

In adaptive leadership theory, Ronald Heifetz and his colleagues argue that in complex environments, leaders must resist the urge to provide technical answers and instead *"give the work back to the people,"* mobilizing them to confront adaptive challenges themselves.[28] In that context, inquiry becomes a primary tool for navigating uncertainty.

Organizational psychologist Edgar Schein argues that *"humble inquiry"* is the art of asking instead of telling and that this posture builds trust and openness in teams.[11] By lowering status barriers and replacing certainty with curiosity, leaders create the conditions for psychological safety and more effective collaboration.

Finally, Brené Brown's research on vulnerability further reinforces this shift. She argues that courageous leadership requires embracing uncertainty rather than armoring up with false certainty, and that this openness fosters trust and connection.[36]

In other words, the smartest thing I did as a new manager wasn't to prove I had the answers, it was to admit I did not and to start asking better questions.

Curiosity Is a Leadership Skill

As mentioned before in this book, we often confuse leadership with certainty. We think that the person in charge is the one with the clearest plan, the sharpest strategy, and the best answers. It sounds reassuring, it feels efficient and it gives the illusion of control.

But when we look at real teams doing real work, the most effective leaders are rarely the ones to speak first. They're rarely the ones who dominate the room with answers. Instead, they're the ones who ask better questions.

The belief that leadership is about knowing what to say and saying it confidently is deeply ingrained in Western corporate culture. It was shaped in the early days of industrial organizations, where hierarchy, predictability, and command structures were necessary for scale. Simplicity was rewarded, clarity was equated with control and the loudest voice often won. Over time we have internalized that model as "real leadership." And to this day, we still carry that blueprint.

But the conditions that shaped that leadership model no longer define our work. We have moved from industrial scale production to complex, knowledge based collaboration. Most organizations operate in ambiguity, strategy shifts quickly, information is distributed and problems are rarely technical and isolated, they're adaptive and interconnected. Teams work across functions, geographies, and expertise areas and in a matrix structure, no single person holds the full picture. In that environment, certainty becomes fragile, answers expire quickly and leadership based solely on authority begins to crack.

In that context, asking questions becomes more powerful than giving answers.

Asking questions is not a passive act, it's a leadership discipline. It requires practice, it requires restraint and it requires emotional regulation. Staying curious when your ego wants to prove itself is hard work, especially for those of us who have fought to earn our seat at the table. And especially for those who already feel scrutinized. For many of us, asking questions can feel dangerous. It can feel like exposing gaps rather than demonstrating strength and it can trigger the fear that we do not belong.

But that discomfort is often the doorway to real leadership.

Choosing inquiry over certainty is a conscious act. It means slowing down before reacting, it means listening before fixing, it means tolerating ambiguity long enough for better thinking to emerge and it means trusting that intelligence is distributed in the room, not concentrated in one person.

Research supports this shift.

Research by Alison Wood Brooks and colleagues shows that people who ask more questions, particularly follow-up questions, are perceived as more responsive and are better liked by their conversation partners.[37] Inquiry signals attention, it signals engagement and it signals that the other person matters.

Organizational psychologist Edgar Schein has long argued that *"humble inquiry"*, the practice of asking instead of telling, builds trust, lowers status barriers, and creates the conditions for psychological safety.[11] When leaders replace certainty with curiosity, they create environments where people feel safe to speak up, challenge assumptions, and contribute more fully.

In fast paced corporate environments, pausing to ask a thoughtful question can feel inefficient, even risky, especially in front of executives or people who intimidate you. But curiosity does not slow progress, it sharpens it. It prevents teams from solving the wrong problem quickly, it ensures alignment before acceleration and it builds shared ownership instead of dependency.

As a leader, your questions shape the room. They signal what matters, they signal what is safe to say out loud, they signal whose perspectives count and they distribute power.

When you consistently ask, *"What are we missing?"* or *"Who else needs to be part of this conversation?"* you are not stepping back from leadership, you are redefining it.

You don't need all the answers, but you do need to protect and cultivate your curiosity. You need to genuinely believe that the people around you hold insights you don't possess and that belief changes the way you show up. It shifts your presence from *"I will fix this"* to *"We will figure this out."*

And that shift is not softness, it's strategic, it's inclusive, it's sustainable and it's leadership.

When We Stop Trying to Have the Answer

When Satya Nadella became CEO of Microsoft in 2014, the company was still a global leader, but internally it was struggling with what he later described as a *"know-it-all"* culture. In *Hit Refresh*, Nadella reflects on a corporate environment that rewarded internal competition over collaboration and certainty over curiosity.[2]

What Nadella brought into Microsoft's leadership was not just strategy, it was humility. Instead of stepping in with assertive mandates to prove he was the right person for the job, he chose to listen. In meetings, he asked questions. Sometimes simple ones and sometimes uncomfortable ones. Questions like, *"What's getting in the way?" "What are we learning?" "Where might we be wrong?"*

That shift may sound subtle, but culturally it was radical.

The change in Microsoft wasn't immediate or fast. At first, people hesitated to follow his lead as they had been conditioned by years of being rewarded for confidence and penalized for doubt. Nadella kept asking his questions and he did so not to trap or test his team, but because he was genuinely curious and wanted to understand what was happening, why and how. He wasn't there to be an oracle who would give everyone the secret path forward, but he was there to build a company that could think, adapt and solve problems together.

And slowly, over time the culture began to shift and people started speaking up. Not just managers, but also engineers and developers. Not just extroverts, but also introverts who had been quietly observing for years without saying much. And everyone did so because someone at the top made it feel safe to think out loud, to ask questions, to be uncertain, to be curious and to not have all the answers. Nadella didn't transform Microsoft by having all the answers and telling everyone where to go, he transformed it by creating space for people to feel safe to ask better questions.

Harvard Business School professor Amy Edmondson's research on psychological safety offers another lens on this shift.[38] In her work, she demonstrates that high-performing teams are not defined by individual brilliance, but by whether people feel safe to speak up, question assumptions, and admit uncertainty. Psychological safety does not emerge automatically, it is shaped by leader behavior. When leaders model curiosity instead of certainty, they signal that it is acceptable to think out loud, to challenge ideas, and to contribute without fear of embarrassment or punishment. Curiosity, in that sense, becomes a structural intervention, not just a personal trait.

I used to believe that not knowing something was a weakness, especially in leadership. I believed asking too many questions would expose uncertainty and diminish my credibility. I also believed that changing my mind would signal inconsistency, as if strong leadership meant holding a position firmly and defending it at all costs.

For me, years of masking reinforced these beliefs deeply. When you spend so much time and energy trying to blend in, the last thing you want to do is draw attention to yourself by admitting you don't understand, by asking questions that reveal you see things differently, or by revising your opinion once new information emerges. Doing so can feel like proof that you don't fully fit in and that you might not deserve to be there in the first place. For those reasons, leading through genuine curiosity didn't just feel uncomfortable, it felt threatening.

What I have learned over the years, and through stories like Satya Nadella's, is that questions don't weaken your position or diminish your credibility. They strengthen it. Questions humanize leadership, they invite others in and they open the door to knowledge, insight, and perspectives you could never access alone. And when you are willing to let those perspectives shape you, even change your mind, you signal something far more powerful than certainty. You signal growth.

Questions shift the center of gravity from power to trust. They make it possible for others to contribute without fear. They make it possible for you to evolve without shame. In that way, curiosity is not just about inquiry, it is about intellectual humility and the courage to update your thinking when reality demands it.

The belief that leaders must always have the answers is a trap. It keeps leaders stuck in performance mode, focused on appearing competent rather than enabling real competence in their teams. A leader who clings to certainty closes the field of possibility and a leader who admits they don't know, who asks, listens, and is willing to change their mind when necessary, creates the conditions for collaboration, creativity, and growth.

More often than not, that begins with a single, sincere question.

Tips and Tools: How to Practice Curiosity-Led Leadership

You don't need a script to ask better questions but you need intention and to have the mindset to do so. Asking better questions takes practice and time to build it into a habit. Here are practical tools to help you do that:

1. Ask Open Questions, Not Leading Ones

Many leaders think they're asking questions when in reality they're making statements with a question mark at the end. These leading questions push people towards agreement instead of genuine and honest reflections. If you want to build trust and insight, shift from leading questions to open questions.

Instead of:
"Don't you think the plan makes sense?"
Ask:
"How do you see this approach working?"

Instead of:
"Isn't this the only realistic option we have?"
Ask:
"What other options might we be overlooking?"

Instead of:
"Wouldn't it be better if we just followed the usual process?"
Ask:
"What process do you think would work best here and why?"

Instead of:
"You agree with this timeline, right?"
Ask:
"What concerns do you have about this timeline?"

Open questions usually start with *what, how* or *tell me more*. They don't offer a direct answer to the person being asked and they don't trap the person into confirming the requester's opinion. When you ask an open question, you send the clear signal that you value dialogue over validation and this signals trust.

The next time you're in a meeting, take the time to notice how many questions being asked are leading questions versus open questions. I strongly recommend writing down some of the leading questions asked and practicing reframing them into genuine open questions. And then start actively using those, you'll rapidly see how quickly the tone of the conversations change when we ask open questions.

2. Build a Question Bank

Curiosity doesn't mean improvising everything in the moment.

The leaders I admire most don't walk into rooms empty handed. They walk in prepared, not with scripts, but with a mindset. And part of that mindset is having a few strong, thoughtful questions ready when conversations get tense, rushed, or superficial.

Preparing a bank of questions can help you walk into rooms prepared and ready to ask open ended questions and lead with curiosity. A question bank is not about memorizing lines, it's about preparing yourself to resist the default of yes or no questions when pressure rises.

Here are examples you can adapt:

In one-to-ones:

- *"What's something slowing you down that I might not see?"*
- *"What's one thing I could do differently that would make your work easier?"*
- *"What part of your work gives you energy right now?"*
- *"If you could redesign one part of your role, what would you change?"*

In team meetings:

- *"What are we missing?"*
- *"If we weren't already committed to this path, what would we choose today?"*
- *"Whose perspective have we not heard yet?"*
- *"What assumptions are we making that could turn out to be wrong?"*

In project reviews:

- *"What worked well this time that we should repeat?"*
- *"What would we do differently next time?"*
- *"Where did luck play a role in our success or failure?"*
- *"What did we learn that others should know?"*

In moments of tension or conflict:

- *"Help me understand what matters most to you here."*
- *"What would a good outcome look like from your perspective?"*
- *"What feels non-negotiable to you here?"*
- *"If we zoomed out six months from now, what would you want to see resolved?"*

In coaching conversations:

- *"What options are you considering?"*
- *"What feels like the biggest stretch for you right now?"*
- *"What support would help you take the next step?"*
- *"What would you try if failure wasn't on the table?"*

Over time, your question bank can become second nature. You don't need to carry these around in a note book or in your phone notes app. The goal here isn't to memorize a list but to truly build the habit of reaching for questions that expand the conversation, create trust and spark thinking. Leaders who rely on statements usually end up doing all the talking. Leaders who rely on questions end up doing the real work of leadership which is to draw the best out of others. Leadership is to be in service to others.

3. Wait Longer Than Feels Comfortable

Most people, leaders included, underestimate silence. The moment a question is asked, many of us expect an answer and we often find ourselves uncomfortable in the silence that follows if answers aren't given immediately. When no one answers straight away, our instincts are to jump back in, reframe the question or to answer it ourselves. Sadly, this impatience often cuts off the knowledge and the insights the question was meant to uncover.

For many people, especially neurodivergents, introverts or non-traditional thinkers, a pause isn't a hesitation, it's actually processing. During this pause they're thinking carefully before speaking, they might be weighing their words, pros and cons, connecting the dots, mapping various scenarios with probabilities, etc. If we rush to fill in the silence, we lose the chance to hear their perspective.

Therefore, a simple practice is to silently count to five after asking a question. More if you can although it might feel uncomfortably long at first. That extra space signals that you're not only asking but also waiting, meaning that you genuinely want an answer and you're not just asking without caring for what people will have to say.

You can even make the pause explicit. You can say *"I'll give everyone a minute to think before we discuss"* or *"Take your time, I want to hear your thoughts."* This creates psychological safety for those who don't jump instantly to answer and who need time to reflect. By doing this, they know their processing time is accepted and welcomed. This makes them also more inclined to share their thoughts.

Finally, remember that great questions need air to breathe. The best leaders aren't only good at asking questions, they're also good at waiting for answers.

4. Name the Risk of Speaking Up

At times, people hesitate to answer questions and silence isn't always because people lack ideas or need more time to process, in some cases, the hesitation is driven by fear. Fear of being wrong, fear of sounding unprepared or fear of saying something that might be judged negatively. In many organizations, the fear is well learned and part of the invisible culture, especially if people have seen colleagues being shut down or criticized for speaking up. Therefore, people rather stay quiet than take the risk of sharing their views.

As a leader, you can change this fear and lower the barrier by naming it directly. Acknowledging the risk of answering straight on is a great way to establish trust and build psychological safety. Keeping the risk unnamed and unacknowledged only reinforces the fear itself. In order to name the risk and the fear directly, you can say *"There are no wrong answers here. We're just exploring this together,"* or *"This is about learning, not about being right,"* or in an even more direct way, which I personally prefer, *"I know it's scary to answer because you don't want to be wrong or judged or penalized for speaking up, but none of that will happen. All answers are welcomed."* By naming the risk out loud, you give people the opportunity to step into the conversation without being pressured to be right or perfect.

It's also important to say that acknowledging the risk doesn't mean lowering the bar when it comes to the quality of the answer and of the discussion. It simply means to create a space where people feel safe enough to engage and contribute, even if their ideas are only half-formed. And this is important because those half-formed ideas could spark other ideas, which in turn could lead to breakthroughs.

Real curiosity requires psychological safety and when people know they won't be punished for trying, they're a lot more likely to share what they think.

5. Listen Like It Matters, Because It Does

Nothing diminishes trust faster than asking a question and then signaling that you actually don't care about the answers. We have all faced this situation where you are asked something and as you answer, you realize that the person who asked isn't listening and they don't care about what you think. You're just wasting your breath. The person who asked is looking at their phone, glazing at their watch or mentally preparing for their answer back or their next point. All of these signal clearly that the answer being given isn't important.

Listening is the other half of asking a question. If you invite someone in, you owe it to them to give them the attention they deserve and that means putting distractions aside, looking at the person who's speaking the best way you can while respecting yourself and your own comfort (not everyone can look at people speaking for a long time) and it means to signal with your body language that you're present. This also means to resist the urge to interrupt or jump in with your own answers.

It also means reflecting back on what you heard when people gave you their answers. You can use sentences like *"What I hear you saying is..."* or *"It sounds like what matters most to you is..."*. Using such phrases shows that you're not only listening but that you value their perspective enough to repeat it and make sure you understood it correctly. Sometimes, even using a simple sentence like *"Tell me more..."* is enough to make people feel seen and heard, which is critical when we ask questions.

In short, when leaders listen like it matters and are fully present, people feel it. They feel seen, respected and trusted and that feeling becomes the foundation for all good forms of collaboration.

Listening habits that build trust:

- Put your phone away and close your laptop during important conversations
- If you can, hold eye contact and nod to show you're following as much as it feels comfortable to you
- Take notes, not to interrupt, but to remember and respect what's being said
- Summarize back key points to confirm understanding
- Ask follow-up questions instead of rushing to give your own view

Visual Summary

Practice	What It Looks Like	Why It Works
1. Ask Open Questions, Not Leading Ones	Replacing statements disguised as questions with genuine what and how prompts. Shifting from "You agree, right?" to "How do you see this?"	Builds trust. Encourages honest reflection instead of compliance. Signals dialogue over validation.
2. Build a Question Bank	Preparing thoughtful questions for 1:1s, meetings, reviews, conflict, and coaching. Walking into conversations ready to expand thinking instead of closing it.	Keeps curiosity intentional under pressure. Prevents defaulting to yes or no questions. Distributes ownership and insight across the team.
3. Wait Longer Than Feels Comfortable	Counting silently before speaking again. Allowing silence to stretch. Explicitly giving people time to think.	Creates space for deeper processing. Includes introverts and reflective thinkers. Unlocks higher quality contributions.
4. Name the Risk of Speaking Up	Acknowledging fear of being wrong. Separating exploration from evaluation. Inviting half-formed ideas without punishment.	Lowers psychological barriers. Increases participation. Builds psychological safety and shared trust.
5. Listen Like It Matters, Because It Does	Removing distractions. Reflecting back what you hear. Asking follow-up questions instead of interrupting or defending.	Demonstrates respect. Deepens understanding. Turns curiosity into real connection and collaboration.

Micro-Practice: Replace One Answer with One Question

In your next conversation, choose one moment where you would normally give advice, direction, or an answer. Instead of responding with your solution, pause and ask one open question from your question bank.

For example, the next time a teammate gives you an update, ask:
"What's one thing that could make this easier?"

Then do three things:

1. Pause silently count to five before saying anything else.
2. Listen fully without interrupting or reframing.
3. Reflect back what you heard: "What I hear you saying is..."

After the conversation, take one minute to reflect:

- Did the other person think more deeply?
- Did they take more ownership?
- Did you feel the urge to jump in and fix it?
- What happened when you resisted that urge?

This practice is not about asking perfect questions, it's about interrupting your reflex to provide answers.

One question. One pause. One moment of restraint.

That is how curiosity becomes a habit.

Practical Quick Phrases

Great questions do more than move a conversation forward. They change the energy in the room, they signal curiosity instead of control and they invite ownership instead of compliance.

When you feel the urge to give direction, try reaching for one of these instead:

- *"What are we assuming that might not be true?"*
- *"What would success look like from your perspective?"*
- *"What's one thing we could simplify here?"*
- *"If we had to decide today, what would we choose?"*
- *"What might we learn if we slowed down for a moment?"*
- *"What do you need from me to move forward?"*

Checklist: What Will You Try This Week?

Curiosity does not become a leadership skill simply because you decided to be curious, it becomes a skill through repetition. Choose one or two of the actions below and practice them deliberately this week.

- Start building a question bank for 1:1s, meetings, and retrospectives.
- Experiment with pausing longer after asking questions.
- Enter one meeting with curiosity as your primary intention, not direction.
- Make it explicit that exploration is welcome before asking for input.
- Reflect back what you heard before sharing your own view.
- Notice when you default to a leading question and consciously reframe it into an open one.
- End one conversation this week by asking, *"What's a question I should be asking you?"*

You don't need to do all of this. Pick one or two and practice consistently. Leadership shifts through small behavioral changes repeated over time.

Closing: Leadership That Begins with Listening

The best leaders are not the ones with the most polished and immediate answers, but the ones who know how to ask generous questions and who are willing to sit with what emerges from them.

When we shift from solution-driven leadership to a leadership style rooted in inquiry, something fundamental changes. We stop centering leadership around individual certainty and start centering it around collective intelligence. We stop equating authority with control and begin to understand that influence often comes from shaping the conditions in which others can think, speak, and contribute freely. The questions we ask determine what receives attention, what feels safe to voice, and whose perspectives are welcomed into the room.

This is not passive leadership, and it is not about avoiding responsibility or difficult decisions, it's about leading in a way that reflects the complexity of modern work. In environments where no single person holds the full picture, asking thoughtful questions and listening carefully to the answers is not a retreat from leadership, it's how leadership happens. It's how direction emerges without domination and how clarity forms without shutting down quieter voices.

For those of us who don't naturally fit the traditional leadership mold, this matters deeply. If you're not the loudest voice, the most charismatic presence, or the quickest to respond, you may have been conditioned to believe that you're somehow leading at a disadvantage. But curiosity is not a secondary skill and listening is not a lesser form of authority. When you ask sincere questions and make space for others to think, you're not compensating for what you lack, you're exercising a different kind of leadership strength.

I've seen this not only in theory, but in the lived reality of messy meetings, difficult 1:1s, and moments where no clear plan was available. For a long time, I believed that my value as a leader depended on how quickly I could respond and how confidently I could defend a position. I believed that changing my mind signaled instability, and that asking too many questions might expose uncertainty in ways that would diminish my credibility. Those beliefs were shaped by years of trying to fit in and trying not to stand out for the wrong reasons.

But what I've learned is that curiosity doesn't threaten authority, it refines it. Changing your mind in light of new information is not inconsistency, it's intellectual integrity. And admitting that you don't yet know is not a sign that you should not be leading, it's often a sign that you are leading responsibly.

When I stopped needing to be the person with all the answers and became the person who asked, *"What do you think we should try?"* the dynamic in the room shifted. Ownership increased, conversations deepened and ideas surfaced that would have remained hidden if I had rushed to fill the silence. By asking and truly listening, I was not stepping back from leadership, I was stepping into it.

Part 2 of this book is about *how we lead*. And sometimes how we lead is not by speaking first, but by listening first. It's not by asserting certainty and authority, but by inviting others to share their perspective. And it's not by proving we belong, but by creating space where others feel that they belong too.

If you feel the pressure that comes with not always knowing what to do, pause. Instead of scrambling for the perfect answer, ask one sincere question and allow the silence to stretch long enough for someone else to enter the conversation. Trust that your leadership is not diminished by your willingness to listen, to learn, and, when necessary, to change your mind. In many cases, it's strengthened by it.

Because in the end, leadership is less about certainty and more about courage.

Rule 5: Boundaries Are Culture

"No is a complete sentence."
Anne Lamott

For a long time, I believed that being a good professional meant being available. Not occasionally, but always. I answered emails late at night even when they could have waited until morning. I said yes to projects I didn't have the bandwidth for because I didn't want to appear difficult or uncommitted. I reshuffled family plans to accommodate work trips that had been suggested as opportunities. On the surface, it looked like dedication, but internally, it felt like pressure that never fully left my body.

At the time, I didn't see it as a boundary issue, I saw it as drive and responsibility. I told myself that once things slowed down, once the next milestone passed, once the next promotion was secured, it would probably rebalance. I framed exhaustion as a temporary phase rather than a structural problem. But of course, things never slowed down. The workload didn't shrink and the expectations didn't soften. What I didn't fully understand was that my behavior wasn't neutral, it was instructional.

Every late email I sent signaled urgency, every unnecessary yes signaled availability and every time I deprioritized myself, I taught the people around me what professionalism and leadership looked like. And because I had fought hard to be taken seriously, I rarely questioned the pattern. I equated being needed with being valuable, being busy as being relevant and being stretched thin with being ambitious.

People learn how they can treat you from what you allow, and as a leader, your actions don't just affect you, they quietly define what becomes acceptable for everyone else. Culture is rarely built through strategy decks or carefully worded values statements. It's built through repetition, through behavior and through what gets rewarded and what gets tolerated. It's built in the quiet moments when no one announces a policy change, but everyone notices what the leader models.

Arianna Huffington's story illustrates this on a much larger scale.

Arianna Huffington is best known as the co-founder of an important online media company The Huffington Post, which was one of the world's first major online news platforms. By the mid-2000s, she was one of the most influential women in the United States and a high profile media entrepreneur.

In 2007, Huffington collapsed at work in her office. She hit her head on the desk as she fell and in the fall broke her cheekbone. She didn't collapse because she was sick in the traditional sense of the term. The cause? Exhaustion and burnout.[39] She had been working eighteen hours per day building her online media platform, answering emails around the clock, attending meetings and never resting enough. At that time, over twenty years ago, overworking wasn't just the norm, it was a leadership style, her leadership style.

The fall in her office became a wake-up call. In interviews, Huffington talked about how she had bought into the collective delusion that burnout was the price we had to pay for success.[40] She realized that by pushing herself past her limits, she wasn't only exhausting herself, she was sending a message to everyone who worked at *The Huffington Post*. She was modeling what she expected leadership to look like and what employees should tolerate. She was reinforcing the idea that work came before health and that constant availability was proof of commitment.

This realization changed everything for Huffington. Following the accident, she began to publicly challenge the corporate culture of overworking, the culture that glorifies constant hustling and working 18 hours per day. She started to advocate for sleep, rest and clear boundaries, not just as a personal wellness strategy, but as an overall leadership strategy for all leaders. She argued that boundaries and health were part of responsible leadership and that corporate culture needed to change. Eventually, she stepped down from her role at *The Huffington Post* to launch *Thrive Global*, a company dedicated to changing the way we work and live.

Arianna Huffington's story is a great reminder that boundaries aren't just about self-care. They're a leadership responsibility and they are foundational to culture. When leaders ignore their own limits and neglect their health, they signal that this is what's expected. By doing so they normalize overextension. But when leaders model rest, clarity and self-respect, they quietly rewrite the rules for everyone watching.

Leadership isn't only about what we achieve, it's about what we normalize.

How You Show Up Becomes the Standard You Set

Boundaries aren't a soft skill, they're a leadership skill. And yet in many corporate environments, the absence of boundaries is still treated as a signal of strength rather than a warning sign. We glorify the employee who answers emails at midnight, the executive whose calendar is stacked with back to back meetings from morning to evening and the leader who brags about functioning on minimal sleep because the job matters more. In too many organizations, overworking continues to be framed as ambition, constant availability as commitment and exhaustion as proof that you care enough.

But culture is not shaped by what we praise in theory, it is shaped by what we normalize in practice.

As a leader, how you show up, how you act and how you behave teaches others what's expected. You become the norm that orients people around you. Not slides you present, but the behavior you exhibit. That's what sets the tone. If you say that you value balance but never take a lunch break and send emails at odd hours, people will believe that breaks are optional and balance is something you say but don't endorse. If you insist there's no pressure to work on weekends but send a Sunday night email that requires a response before Monday morning, some people will feel they have to mirror that behavior in order to be perceived as dedicated and competent.

Leadership is always instructional, even when you don't intend for it to be.

For a long time, I worked with an executive who regularly left early to pick up their kids or take them to swim class. They didn't disengage from their role, and they certainly didn't lack ambition, but they were clear about how their day was structured and what mattered. They adjusted their schedule accordingly and worked again later in the evening when necessary, but they never imposed that rhythm on the rest of us. And what struck me most was not the logistics of their schedule, but the clarity of it. There was no apology attached to it, no performative busyness to compensate for leaving early, no over explaining. They simply integrated leadership and life in a way that felt aligned for them.

My own team noticed, they commented on how powerful it was to see someone at that level visibly prioritize family while still delivering results. That single behavior communicated more about what was acceptable than any formal policy ever could. It gave others permission to structure their own days in sustainable ways and made it clear that outcomes mattered more than performative presence.

This lesson is echoed beyond my own experience. *In Becoming*, Michelle Obama writes about her time as an executive at the University of Chicago Hospitals and the rule she held firmly: she left work to be home for dinner with her children every day.[41] She did so without apology and without disguising it. Rather than hiding her boundaries, she made them visible. In doing so, she demonstrated that commitment to work and commitment to family weren't mutually exclusive. Her clarity did not diminish her credibility, it reinforced it, and it offered a powerful example of how leaders can model what they value.

Boundaries, in that sense, are not about control but about clarity. They communicate what is sustainable, what is protected and what will not be quietly sacrificed in the name of urgency. They say, *"This is what I can give, this is what I won't compromise and this is how I work."* When leaders articulate and model those limits consistently, they reduce ambiguity and create psychological stability for the people around them.

I wrote about this in a blog post titled *Stop Negotiating With Myself*, where I reflected on a pattern that had quietly shaped much of my professional life.[42] I noticed how often I would renegotiate my own limits in order to avoid discomfort. I would agree to requests I didn't have the bandwidth for, accept projects outside my scope and stay silent when I wanted to push back, all because saying yes felt safer than risking disappointment. On the surface, it looked like flexibility and commitment. In reality, it was self-abandonment. Every time I negotiated against my own limits, I signaled, both to myself and to others, that those limits were optional. When leaders treat their own boundaries as negotiable, the culture around them begins to do the same. And when leaders are unclear about their own limits, their teams struggle to understand expectations. Over time, that confusion breeds resentment and burnout.

Leadership without boundaries isn't generosity, it's depletion. And depletion is contagious.

There is empirical support for this as well. A study published in the *Journal of Applied Psychology* found that employees who were better able to psychologically detach from work during non-work hours experienced lower emotional exhaustion and improved well-being.[43] The research also showed that frequent work related communication outside of work hours made detachment more difficult. In other words, boundaries are not merely personal preferences, they directly influence recovery, energy and long-term sustainability at work.

Similarly, Gallup's 2022 workplace research shows that only two in ten employees strongly agree that their well-being is prioritized at work.[44] The gap between stated values and lived experience is wide. While reports and mission statements often speak about well-being, employees ultimately judge culture by daily behavior. When leaders set and respect their own boundaries, they make well-being visible and operational rather than rhetorical.

When you say yes to everything as a leader, you may believe you are being supportive, but what you are actually creating is instability. You signal that urgency overrides judgment and that capacity is infinite. Over time, that ambiguity erodes trust because people can't anchor themselves in consistent expectations.

Boundaries provide structure, they define what excellence looks like without equating it with exhaustion. They create clarity around what is negotiable and what is not and they prevent burnout from becoming the silent cost of ambition.

Your team learns more from what you tolerate than from what you declare. They observe when you respond, they notice when you cancel personal commitments and they register how you react when someone else sets a limit. Whether you intend it or not, your behavior becomes the model to follow.

Boundaries are not barriers to leadership, they're the foundation that makes sustainable leadership possible, because they translate our values into visible behavior and make it clear that ambition doesn't have to come at the expense of our own well-being.

Boundaries Are a Mirror

For a long time, before I'd taken the time to properly reflect on this, I believed that boundaries were about protecting myself from others. I thought boundaries were defensive. They were about saying no, drawing a line and keeping the bad stuff out. They felt reactive rather than intentional and something you put up when things got overwhelming or unfair.

What I didn't understand at the time was that boundaries don't just protect us from others, they reveal something about ourselves. They show what we believe we have to tolerate in order to belong. They expose the quiet bargains we make with ourselves to stay relevant, to stay liked and to stay considered for the next opportunity. When we repeatedly override our own limits, we're not simply being flexible, we're communicating, both internally and externally, that our needs are negotiable. In that sense, boundaries are not walls we build against the world, they are reflections of how we position ourselves within it.

Over time, and after realizing that my leadership style was quietly exhausting me, I began to see that boundaries reflect what we believe we're worth. Because when I said yes to everything, every request, every late night email, every last minute weekend slide deck, I wasn't being generous or ambitious or proving my value, I was afraid. I was afraid to disappoint, afraid to seem selfish, afraid to lose relevance and afraid that if I wasn't always available, I wouldn't be considered for the next opportunity. I equated being needed with being valued, so I made myself endlessly accessible, turning availability into my currency and convincing myself that the more I gave, the safer my position would be. What I didn't acknowledge at the time was that this currency came at a cost, and that the price I was paying was my energy, my clarity and, eventually, my health.

Like Arianna Huffington, burnout eventually came knocking at my door. Not in one dramatic collapse, but slowly, quietly, through exhaustion that I normalized and stress that I minimized. I told myself that this was just what leadership required and that this was the price of ambition. I told myself that once I had secured the next milestone, I could recalibrate, but the recalibration never came.

There is a quiet conditioning that many of us carry, especially women, neurodivergent people, people of color and anyone raised to please. Many of us have internalized the belief that worth is measured in output and that our value increases the more we can endure without complaint. We learn that being agreeable keeps us safe, that being accommodating makes us likable and that saying no makes us difficult.

And when that conditioning travels with us into leadership, it becomes cultural.

Clinical psychologist Dr. Thema Bryant writes in *Homecoming* about how early relational conditioning can teach people to equate love and belonging with over-functioning and self-sacrifice, making it difficult to set healthy boundaries later in life.[45] Similarly, Dr. Nedra Glover Tawwab argues in *Set Boundaries, Find Peace* that boundaries are not selfish, but necessary for healthy relationships, and that when they're absent, resentment and emotional exhaustion often follow.[46]

When I began to understand this, I saw that my reluctance to set boundaries wasn't rooted in generosity, it was rooted in fear. And fear doesn't build healthy cultures.

When I finally started saying no more often to things that drained me, to meetings that could have been emails, to projects where I couldn't genuinely add value and to initiatives that didn't align with our priorities, something unexpected happened. I didn't become less respected, I didn't become irrelevant and I didn't become difficult. Instead, I became more present, more grounded, more focused and more trustworthy, because people feel safer around someone who knows their limits than around someone who keeps bending them.

And this matters beyond the personal level, because leadership is never contained to the individual. When a leader burns out, and I have been there, the impact rarely stops with them. The team absorbs the heat, they compensate quietly, they step in without being asked and they stretch themselves to cover the gaps. And slowly, often without realizing it, they internalize the pace that was never sustainable to begin with.

Over time, that pace becomes normal. The late nights become expected, the constant availability becomes proof of commitment and the unspoken message settles in: if you want to succeed here, you have to endure.

When we model overextension, we teach our people that exhaustion is the price of ambition and that self neglect is a sign of loyalty. But when we model boundaries, consistently and without apology, we teach something entirely different. We teach that thriving is not a reward waiting at the end of the road, it's part of how we define success from the start. We teach that ambition doesn't require self erosion and that sustainable leadership is not a compromise, it's a choice.

In that sense, boundaries are not personal preferences, they are cultural signals. They shape what becomes normal, what becomes expected and what becomes possible for the people around us.

Brené Brown writes in *Dare to Lead*, *"Clear is kind. Unclear is unkind."*[36] Boundaries are how we get clear, not only with others, but with ourselves. They reduce ambiguity, they reduce emotional leakage, they prevent the slow accumulation of resentment that so often sits underneath burnout. And as we will explore in Rule 6, burnout rarely begins with one catastrophic event, it begins with small moments of self-betrayal repeated over time.

So the next time you feel selfish for holding a boundary, pause. Ask yourself what you are really protecting. Is it your reputation, your image, your desire to be indispensable? Or is it your energy, your integrity and your humanity?

Because leadership doesn't begin with sacrifice, it begins with clarity. And clarity starts with the boundaries you are willing to honor.

Tips and Tools: How to Lead with Clear Boundaries

Boundaries aren't a sign of weakness, instead they should be considered leadership tools. They help you stay grounded, communicate clearly, and model what healthy culture at work looks like.

Here are five practical ways to lead with clear boundaries:

1. Define Your Non-Negotiables

Boundaries rarely collapse because we don't care about them, they collapse because they're vague.

If you haven't clearly defined what is non-negotiable for you, you will renegotiate it in moments of pressure. And such pressure always comes whether it's a last-minute request, a senior stakeholder asking for *"just a quick favor."* or a deadline that suddenly shifts. When your limits are unclear to you, they become flexible to everyone else.

Start by identifying two or three non-negotiables that protect your energy, your focus, and your long-term sustainability. Not ten and not an aspirational list of everything you wish you did better. Two or three anchors that make it possible for you to lead without eroding yourself.

These might look like:

- No meetings before a certain hour because that's when you do your best thinking
- Protecting two hours of uninterrupted focus time each day
- Not checking email after a specific time
- Blocking time for exercise, therapy, or family without apology

The point is not rigidity, it's clarity.

Ask yourself:

- What consistently drains me in a typical week?
- When do I do my clearest thinking?
- What helps me reset instead of slowly accumulate stress?
- Where do I tend to negotiate against myself?
- What habit, if protected, would make everything else easier?

Your non-negotiables are not about comfort, they're about capacity. They create the conditions that allow you to show up grounded rather than reactive.

And here is the part many leaders skip: *boundaries don't work in silence*.

If you protect your time but never communicate why, people interpret your absence through their own assumptions. When you name your boundary clearly, you reduce ambiguity and prevent resentment from filling the gaps.

For example:
"I don't check emails after 18:00 because I want to protect that time for my kids. If something is truly urgent, text me."

That sentence does more than protect your evening. It models something cultural. It signals that family time is legitimate, it normalizes limits and it shows that leadership and humanity can coexist.

Leaders who define and communicate their non-negotiables don't just protect themselves, they quietly reset what is considered normal. And culture is built in those quiet resets.

2. Normalize Saying No, or Not Yet

One of the most powerful cultural signals a leader can send is not how enthusiastically they say yes, but how clearly and calmly they say no.

For many of us, especially those who have spent years working hard to be taken seriously, to not be labelled difficult, to not appear uncommitted or overly sensitive, saying no can feel far more threatening than taking on too much. We cushion it in explanations, we wrap it in apologies, we add unnecessary context and reassurance, as if declining a request requires a moral defense. And when that becomes a habit, it subtly communicates that boundaries are conditional and that clarity must be earned through justification.

But a respectful and direct no, or not yet, is not rejection, it's prioritization made visible and it's leadership practiced in real time.

Saying no doesn't mean shutting a door or dismissing an idea. Often it simply means not now, not in this way, or not within our current scope. The framing matters, but so does the tone. When we overexplain or apologize excessively, we signal that we feel guilty for protecting capacity. When we respond with calm clarity, we signal that focus is intentional.

Instead of defending your capacity, try anchoring your response in priorities:

- *"We're at capacity right now. Taking this on now would put other priorities at risk."*
- *"That doesn't align with our current focus. If that changes, we can revisit."*
- *"We don't have the bandwidth for this right now. Let's stay focused on our core commitments."*
- *"That's outside our team's scope. Let's clarify ownership so expectations are clear."*
- *"If we say yes to this, something else needs to move. Which priority are we willing to delay?"*
- *"This has potential, but the timing isn't right. Let's revisit at a later stage."*

Notice that none of these responses attack the idea or the person. They simply make trade-offs explicit. And leadership, especially in complex environments, is often about making trade-offs visible rather than pretending they don't exist.

When leaders normalize thoughtful refusal, the culture shifts in subtle but meaningful ways. The center of gravity moves from overcommitment to understanding, from silent resentment to transparent prioritization, and from proving dedication through exhaustion to demonstrating leadership through focus and clarity. Every time you model a grounded no, you make it safer for someone else to protect their limits too, and over time those repeated moments accumulate into something larger than a single decision. They become culture.

3. Structure Your Availability Instead of Performing It

One of the fastest ways to erode your own focus as a leader is to confuse accessibility with constant availability.

For years, I believed that being a good leader meant being reachable at all times. Every ping and every "quick question" felt like proof that I was needed and therefore useful. But what I didn't account for was the cognitive cost of that pattern. Context switching isn't neutral, it fragments attention and it stretches the nervous system. For those of us who are already sensitive to noise, interruption or overstimulation, it can quietly drain energy long before the day is over.

The intention behind constant availability is often generous. You want your team to feel supported, you want to be approachable and you don't want to create hierarchy through distance. But without structure, accessibility slowly becomes reactivity, and reactivity is not sustainable leadership.

A more intentional alternative is to design your availability instead of performing it.

Borrow a practice from academia and create defined *"office hours"* where your team knows you are fully available for questions, brainstorming, quick approvals or spontaneous support. Outside of those windows, you protect your focus time. Not because you don't care, but because your thinking deserves uninterrupted space.

For example, you might block two hours per week labeled *"drop-in time"* and communicate clearly: *"These are the windows where I'm fully available for questions or quick discussions. Outside of that, I'll be focused on deep work. If something is urgent, please flag it clearly."*

You'll notice two things happen. First, many *"urgent"* interruptions resolve themselves or become better formed questions when people know there is a dedicated space to bring them. Second, your own cognitive clarity improves because you're no longer living in a constant state of micro-disruption.

This is especially important if you are someone who masks, who expends extra energy reading rooms, decoding tone or regulating your own responses in fast paced environments. Unstructured interruption amplifies that cost, structured availability reduces it.

When you model this approach, you teach your team something subtle but powerful: being accessible doesn't require being perpetually on call, leadership doesn't require self fragmentation and focus is not selfish, it is strategic.

Over time, this small structural boundary shifts the culture from one of reactive urgency to one of intentional support. You remain present and helpful, but not at the expense of your own clarity.

And clarity, as we've already seen, is the foundation of sustainable leadership.

4. Model Boundary Language in Meetings

Meetings are often where boundaries disappear first.

Sometimes it shows up in obvious ways. Meetings start late, they run over or the conversation expands far beyond the original purpose and everything suddenly feels urgent. In those moments, if a leader stays silent, the message is clear: time is flexible and people's focus is expendable.

But even in environments where meetings start and end on time, boundaries can erode in more subtle ways. Agendas, if they exist, aren't followed and the purpose of the meeting isn't clearly defined. We shift between brainstorming, alignment and decision making without naming which mode we're in, roles and responsibilities are implied rather than clarified or conversations circle without landing anywhere concrete.

And all of that has a cost. It increases cognitive load, it favors the loudest voices, it leaves quieter thinkers or more reflective contributors behind and it drains energy without producing clarity. Over time, it teaches people that meetings are something to endure rather than something that moves work forward.

As a leader, the way you speak in these moments sets the tone. If you accept scope creep, you normalize it. If you allow unclear ownership, you reinforce it. But if you name boundaries out loud, you model something different: focus, structure and respect for people's time and attention.

Calling out boundaries doesn't have to be harsh or awkward. It can be done with calm, clear language such as:

- *"Let's make sure we end on time so everyone can move to their next commitment."*
- *"What decision are we actually trying to make here?"*

- *"Are we brainstorming or deciding? Let's choose one."*
- *"Who owns the next step so this doesn't get lost?"*
- *"We're running out of time. Which outcome matters most today?"*
- *"I'd like to park this topic and come back when we have the right people in the room."*

When you use this kind of language consistently, you protect more than the clock. You protect focus. you protect clarity, you protect people's mental energy and you show that boundaries are not about rigidity, they're about making sure that work is intentional rather than reactive.

Meetings are cultural classrooms and people learn from how you hold the space. If you model structure, respect and role clarity, others will begin to do the same.

And that's how boundaries move from personal preference to shared practice.

5. Respect Others' Boundaries Visibly

Boundaries don't become cultural norms because they're written into policies, they become norms because they're reinforced in real time.

If someone says no to protect their time, declines a late request or leaves at the end of the workday, your reaction as a leader carries weight. A raised eyebrow, a joke about "part timers," a subtle comment about commitment or even a quiet preference for those who stay longer can undo weeks of messaging about well-being.

More often than we realize, the punishment of boundaries is subtle. It's not formal discipline, it's social signaling. It's who gets praised, who gets promoted and who gets described as *"hungry"* or *"dedicated."* When the people who overextend themselves are celebrated and the people who hold limits are overlooked, the culture learns quickly what truly matters.

And let's be honest, many of us have violated our own boundaries precisely because we were afraid it would impact our career if we didn't. That fear is not irrational, it's learned.

For those of us who already feel different in corporate environments, whether because of neurodivergence, gender, sexuality, culture or temperament, the pressure to overperform is often higher. We may feel that we have less room to say no, less margin for being misunderstood and less tolerance for being perceived as *"not committed enough."* In those environments, visible reinforcement of boundaries is not just supportive, it's protective.

If someone sets a boundary, make your support explicit.

You can say:

- *"Thanks for being clear about your limits."*
- *"I appreciate you protecting your focus time. That helps the whole team."*
- *"Good call ending on time. Let's all respect that."*
- *"Thanks for flagging capacity. That clarity helps us plan better."*

These statements may seem small, but they shift the narrative. They frame boundaries as professional, not personal. They associate clarity with competence and they signal that respecting limits is not career limiting, it's culturally aligned.

When leaders reinforce boundaries out loud, the culture shifts from silent permission to active protection. People begin to believe that they won't be penalized for sustainability and they begin to trust that they don't have to earn belonging through exhaustion.

And over time, that trust becomes the foundation for healthier performance. Because boundaries don't hold unless they're backed by behavior. And one of the most powerful behaviors a leader can model is this: when someone protects their limits, you protect them too.

Visual Summary

Practice	**What It Looks Like**	**Why It Works**
1. Define Your Non-Negotiables	Identify two or three clear limits that protect your energy and focus. Communicate them explicitly instead of assuming people will guess. Example: *"I don't check emails after 18:00. If it's urgent, text me."*	Clarity prevents quiet renegotiation under pressure. When leaders name and hold their anchors, they reduce ambiguity and reset what is considered normal in the culture.

2. Normalize Saying No, or Not Yet	Decline requests calmly and directly without overexplaining. Anchor your response in priorities rather than guilt. Make trade-offs visible.	A grounded no signals focus and intentional leadership. It shifts the culture from overcommitment and silent resentment to transparent prioritization and sustainable performance.
3. Structure Your Availability Instead of Performing It	Create defined windows for questions or support, such as office hours or drop-in time. Protect deep work outside those windows while remaining accessible during them.	Designed availability protects cognitive clarity and reduces reactive leadership. It teaches that accessibility does not require constant interruption.
4. Model Boundary Language in Meetings	Name scope, roles, decisions and time limits explicitly. Ask: "What decision are we making?" or "Who owns the next step?" Close on time and protect focus.	Meetings are cultural classrooms. When leaders model structure and clarity, they reduce cognitive load, protect energy and normalize intentional work instead of reactive urgency.
5. Respect Others' Boundaries Visibly	Publicly reinforce when someone protects their limits. Acknowledge capacity concerns and thank people for clarity. Avoid rewarding overextension.	Boundaries become cultural norms when they are reinforced, not punished. Visible support builds psychological safety and shifts performance from exhaustion to sustainability.

Micro-Practice: Practice a Clean Boundary

Think of one boundary you've been quietly negotiating with yourself. Not a dramatic one, not a career-defining stand, just the small, recurring moment where you tend to bend. The meeting that runs long, the extra request you automatically say yes to or the email you answer even though you told yourself you wouldn't.

When the next opportunity appears, pause before acting. Instead of cushioning your answer with apologies, long justifications or nervous overexplaining, offer a clean response. For example:

"I'm at capacity right now and taking this on would compromise other priorities."

Or:

"I won't be available this evening. Let's continue tomorrow."

Say it calmly. Say it once. Then stop.

Notice what happens internally.
Do you feel the urge to add more context to soften the boundary?
Do you feel tension in your body?
Do you anticipate disappointment that hasn't actually been expressed?

Then observe the response you receive. Very often, the reaction is far less dramatic than the fear that preceded it.

Afterwards, reflect:

- What story did I tell myself about what would happen?
- What actually happened?
- Did clarity weaken my credibility, or did it strengthen it?

This practice is not about becoming rigid or unapproachable. It's about learning that you can be clear without being harsh and firm without being unkind.

And that is where sustainable leadership begins.

Practical Quick Phrases

In moments of pressure, boundaries tend to collapse not because we don't believe in them, but because we hesitate. We search for the perfect wording, we overthink the tone and in that hesitation we often default back to accommodation.

Having a few clear, go-to phrases ready can make all the difference. Not as scripts to hide behind, but as anchors you can rely on when you feel yourself about to renegotiate your own limits. The goal is not to sound polished, it's to stay clear.

Boundaries teach people how to work with you and how to protect themselves, too. These short phrases model clarity and self-respect while keeping collaboration intact. They're not defensive, they're decisive.

- *"I don't check messages after 18:00. If it's urgent, text me."*
- *"I want to give this proper attention, so let's schedule it for tomorrow."*
- *"I don't have the bandwidth for this right now. Who else could take it?"*
- *"Let's end on time so we all have space to reset."*
- *"Thanks for being clear about your limits. That helps everyone."*

Checklist: What Will You Try This Week?

Boundaries become real through practice, not intention. Choose one or two actions below to try this week to start working with your boundaries more consistently.

- Identify your non-negotiables
- Communicate at least one personal boundary to your team
- Say *"No"* or *"Not now"* without overexplaining and without feeling guilty
- Model healthy limits in meetings and/or emails
- Acknowledge a colleague's boundary positively
- Leave time for recovery after intense work
- Block time in your calendar to make sure you're not always available

Closing: Boundaries Are an Act of Leadership, Not Rebellion

There was a time when I believed that saying yes to everything made me a better employee and a better leader. I believed that staying late, answering emails on weekends and stepping in whenever something felt urgent demonstrated commitment and reliability. I thought that availability equaled value and that the more indispensable I made myself, the safer my position would be. What I did not fully grasp at the time was that I was not simply proving dedication, I was quietly teaching everyone around me that my limits were optional.

Leadership is rarely shaped by grand declarations. It's shaped by patterns and the pattern I was modeling was one of constant accommodation. Every time I accepted a last minute meeting without question, every time I shifted personal commitments to accommodate shifting priorities and every time I responded immediately to something that could have waited, I reinforced the idea that urgency overrides boundaries.

There was one afternoon when I had intentionally blocked my calendar to focus on work that required deep thinking. Shortly after, a senior colleague scheduled a last minute alignment meeting during that protected time. My instinct was to accept immediately as I didn't want to appear resistant or inflexible. But before clicking accept, I paused and asked myself whether the meeting truly required that exact time slot. After reviewing the agenda, I realized it could wait.

So I replied that I needed the afternoon to work on deliverables and asked if we could move the discussion to the following day. It felt uncomfortable and my body reacted as if I had done something risky. Yet the response I received was simple: *"Of course."* The meeting moved, nothing collapsed and no negative narrative was built around my commitment.

What struck me afterwards was not the ease of the rescheduling, but the story I had been carrying. I had assumed that protecting my focus would be interpreted as defiance. In reality, it was interpreted as clarity.

This is something Shonda Rhimes reflects on in her memoir *Year of Yes: How to Dance It Out, Stand In the Sun and Be Your Own Person.*[47] Rhimes, the creator and producer behind television series such as *Grey's Anatomy* and *Scandal*, writes about reaching a point where her automatic *"yes"* had become draining rather than expansive. Although the book centers on saying yes to what scared her, it also captures a deeper shift: she became far more intentional about where her energy went and why. That shift required recognizing that not every invitation deserved her presence and that participation without discernment erodes both clarity and capacity. What emerged wasn't diminished influence, but greater alignment. Her yes became meaningful precisely because it was no longer automatic.

Research reinforces this distinction between sustainable contribution and self erasure. In *Give and Take: Why Helping Others Drives Our Success*, organizational psychologist Adam Grant shows that the most successful givers are not those who give indiscriminately, but those who combine generosity with clear priorities and self-protection. He distinguishes between *"selfless givers,"* who often burn out, and *"otherish givers,"* who are generous while still protecting their own goals and energy. Without limits, giving can become depletion. With limits, it becomes sustainable and strategic.[48]

The same pattern shows up in organizational research more broadly. Studies on psychological detachment and recovery demonstrate that employees who are able to mentally disengage from work during non-work hours experience lower emotional exhaustion and stronger well-being over time.[43] The research also shows that frequent work related communication outside working hours makes detachment more difficult. When leaders remain constantly available, they increase the likelihood that others feel compelled to stay cognitively connected as well. By contrast, when leaders visibly protect their own time, they make recovery culturally legitimate rather than quietly discouraged.

These examples, mine, Rhimes' and the research behind them, are not arguments for disengagement, they are arguments for intentional leadership. Boundaries don't signal rebellion, they signal discernment. They communicate that not everything urgent is important and that not every opportunity deserves automatic acceptance.

Over time, I began to see that boundaries are less about protecting time and more about protecting myself. They prevent leadership from becoming a performance of endurance, they ensure that ambition doesn't quietly morph into self neglect and they transform values from abstract statements into visible practice.

So the next time you hesitate before protecting your focus, declining a request or logging off at a defined time, examine the narrative underneath that hesitation. Are you afraid of appearing uncommitted, or are you uncomfortable with no longer measuring your value through overextension? Because leadership is not measured by how much you can absorb without breaking. It's measured by the clarity with which you define what is sustainable and the courage with which you uphold it.

Boundaries are not rebellion against work, they are an acknowledgment that meaningful work requires energy, clarity and limits, and that protecting those limits is part of leading responsibly rather than stepping away from responsibility.

Rule 6: Burnout Is Not a Badge of Honor

"If we want to live a Wholehearted life, we have to become intentional about cultivating sleep and play, and about letting go of exhaustion as a status symbol and productivity as self-worth."
Brené Brown

I once worked for a leader who bragged about only needing to sleep four hours per night and claimed to be more functional when sleeping fewer hours. They proudly showed up to meetings after flying on a red-eye pretending sleep was optional and preached purpose and balance in public, but behind the scenes, operated like a firestarter. They would send urgent emails at odd hours, they would create fires to build momentum and they'd reward employees who ran themselves into the ground.

At the time, I was only starting my corporate career. I wanted to succeed and I wanted to belong so I tried to keep up. I skipped lunch, I stayed up late and because I wanted to do well, I overdelivered. I treated tiredness as a badge of honor and I let myself believe that endurance was a proof of competence. And for a while that worked, I pushed myself hard, I didn't sleep enough and I was praised for my deliveries. But the body, at least my body, doesn't function sustainably on four to six hours of sleep and what was bound to happen happened and I started to get sick a lot. Colds, flus, stomach bugs, one after the other. My concentration vanished and I started to dread Mondays and then Tuesday and then every day. What I had framed as resilience was slowly eroding my health.

Back then, I truly believed that working hard and hustling through was a demonstration of my resilience and the price to pay to prove I belonged. But I wasn't being resilient, I was being complicit in a culture that valued overwork, hustling and burnout.

Psychologist Christina Maslach, who pioneered burnout research, defines burnout as the combination of emotional exhaustion, depersonalization, and a reduced sense of personal accomplishment.[49] Unlike popular belief in many work cultures, burnout isn't just tiredness, it's what happens when demands placed on us consistently exceed our capacity over time. And it can happen even when we're praised, promoted, and publicly rewarded for our performance. Recognition doesn't prevent burnout if the underlying pace remains unsustainable.

And burnout isn't simply a modern complaint attributed to younger generations who supposedly *"want to work less."* Long before today's corporate hustle culture, Carl Jung warned about the psychological risks of over-identifying with the roles we perform. In Two Essays on Analytical Psychology, he described the persona as the social mask we wear to function in society. When we become too entangled in that mask, he argued, we risk losing contact with the deeper self beneath it.[50]

Jung was not writing about burnout as we define it today. But his insight is strikingly relevant to modern work culture. When professional identity becomes fused with personal worth, when performance becomes indistinguishable from selfhood, something begins to erode. Burnout often follows a similar pattern. It drains us until our sense of value is no longer rooted in who we are, but in what we produce.

Too often, when people become burned out, a feeling of shame and guilt accompanies them. They don't just feel tired, they feel as though they have failed. Failed to be strong enough, failed to manage their time better and failed to keep up. The irony is that burnout rarely happens because we're lazy or disengaged. It happens because we care deeply and because we don't know how to stop.

For many introverts, neurodivergent professionals, people with impostor syndrome, or anyone accustomed to proving themselves twice as hard for half the recognition, the risk is even higher. When you already feel slightly outside the mold, slowing down can feel like confirming every doubt. The system was not built with your nervous system in mind, it was built for output, visibility, and speed.

And yet, you still need to pause. Because burnout isn't noble, it's corrosive. Over time, it doesn't just drain energy, it silences the very voices that once brought depth and insight to the room.

And the cost of burnout rarely stays contained within the individual. When leaders operate from depletion, their teams absorb the consequences. Urgency becomes the default tone, patience shortens, decisions become reactive instead of thoughtful and creativity narrows because there is no cognitive space left for reflection. What looks like high performance on the surface is often sustained by invisible strain underneath.

Burnout also distorts leadership judgment. When you are chronically exhausted, everything can begin to feel immediate and equally important. Boundaries blur, and the nervous system remains in a low grade state of threat. In that state, it becomes harder to listen deeply, to tolerate ambiguity, or to respond with steadiness rather than speed.

This is why burnout cannot be dismissed as a personal time management issue. It's a leadership issue and, ultimately, a cultural one. If left unexamined, it quietly becomes the operating system of entire organizations. And once it becomes normal, few people question it until something breaks.

Working to Exhaustion Is Not a Flex

In many corporate environments, somewhere along the way, we turned exhaustion and burnout as proof of commitment. We started treating being tired and overworked as a status symbol. The busier you are, the more valuable you must be.

But burnout isn't a badge of honor, it's a warning sign. And in leadership, it's not just personal, it's contagious. When leaders model depletion as dedication, they set the standard for everyone else. Urgency becomes normal, overextension becomes expected and rest becomes questionable.

This pattern has been publicly visible for years. Former Google and Yahoo executive Marissa Mayer mentioned in interviews that she used to work up to 130 hours per week. She would schedule every minute of her day and sometimes sleep under her desk to keep up. At the time, this kind of exhaustion was celebrated as proof of not only dedication, but also strength. Today, years later, she talks about this as a cautionary tale of how tech culture and corporate life have glorified burnout as a badge of honor and something that needs to be changed.[51]

And this isn't just anecdotal. In 2019, the *World Health Organization* officially recognized burnout as an occupational phenomenon in the *International Classification of Diseases*, defining it as the result of chronic workplace stress that has not been successfully managed.[52] This distinction matters because it shifts the conversation away from personal weakness and toward workplace conditions. Burnout is not laziness or disengagement, it's a signal that something in the environment is unsustainable.

And yet, even with this global recognition that burnout is an *occupational phenomenon*, too many corporate environments continue to value and even admire overwork. Staying late becomes a virtue and working more than 40 hours per week is the norm. People who pause are seen as lacking drive, while those who push through are still celebrated.

While some argue that hustle culture is fading and that employers are becoming more protective of employees' time, recent reporting suggests that the opposite dynamic persists in certain sectors. A 2025 *Wired* article described how some Silicon Valley AI startups are embracing China's controversial "996" work schedule, 9 am to 9 pm, six days a week, even asking candidates during screening whether they are prepared to work those hours.[53]

In *The Burnout Epidemic*, Jennifer Moss critiques what she describes as a culture of resilience that expects employees not only to keep going, but to do so without visible strain. [54] In such environments, the ability to endure in silence becomes a marker of commitment.

The consequences of overwork are not abstract. A 2021 joint report by the *World Health Organization* and the *International Labor Organization* found that people working 55 hours or more per week face a 35 percent higher risk of stroke and a 17 percent higher risk of heart disease compared to those working standard hours.[55] Exhaustion may be culturally rewarded, but the body doesn't interpret it as strength.

In short, working to exhaustion isn't a flex nor is it leadership, it's self-neglect in a culture that masks harm as hustle and commitment.

Former Starbucks CEO Howard Schultz has reflected honestly on the toll that relentless work took during the company's hyper-growth and turnaround years. In his memoir Onward, he writes about the all-consuming nature of driving strategy through constant urgency and pressure, and how sustaining that pace put strain on his own well-being and relationships. Schultz describes periods when the business felt like it was operating in crisis mode and everything demanded immediate attention. In interviews and public conversations about the book, he has acknowledged that those years taught him hard lessons about balance, perspective and the cost of equating busyness with worth.[56]

Rather than portraying that intensity as proof of commitment, his later reflections emphasize the necessity of stepping back and of creating space to see more clearly what actually matters. He articulates a shift in his thinking from viewing perpetual motion as indispensable to recognizing that stepping away, resting and recalibrating are essential not only for personal health but also for sustaining good leadership over time. His experience illustrates a broader pattern: leaders who chase performance at all costs often pay a personal price in health, connection and presence, only realizing too late that the myth of indispensability was costing them what truly mattered.

Burnout isn't just personal, it's systemic. When leaders push past their own limits, they model that behavior for their teams. Over time, exhaustion becomes normalized and the emotional distance that accompanies burnout erodes trust, clarity and psychological safety. In *The Burnout Fix*, Dr. Jacinta Jiménez emphasizes that leaders play a critical role in shaping workplace norms, and that sustainable success requires modeling recovery, boundaries and self-regulation rather than relentless output.[57] Cultures that normalize overwork don't become stronger, they become fragile.

So if we want to build teams that thrive, that innovate, where trust is fostered, we have to stop romanticizing collapse. We have to stop calling burnout as ambition and we have to stop treating rest as a luxury. Rest isn't an indulgence, it's maintenance and without it, nothing we build can last.

You Were Never Meant to Run on Empty

Burnout doesn't always announce itself with a dramatic collapse like it did for Arianna Huffington. In most cases, it seeps through the cracks over time, slowly and quietly. First, it looks like stress, you reread emails five times before understanding them, you lie in bed at night with your mind racing, you feel guilty for taking a break or even leaving on time. Burnout also creeps into your relationships. Your body is present when you come home but your mind is still in a PowerPoint or in your inbox. Burnout steals your patience and you become snappy at the people you love. You stop laughing, you stop being fully present and slowly exhaustion hollows you until all that's left is performance without any presence.

This is not just my story, it's the story of millions of professionals. According to Gallup's *2023 State of the Global Workplace Report*, 44 percent of employees worldwide said they experienced a lot of stress at work in recent days.[58] Other research shows that burnout risk is even higher for women, caregivers and neurodivergent professionals who are navigating high-pressure environments that reward urgency and availability over boundaries and sustainability.

Across Europe, similar trends appear. In 2022, the *European Agency for Safety and Health at Work* published a report that stated that half the workers consider stress common in their workplace and that stress, depression and anxiety account for more than half of all lost working days.[59] Even in regions that are praised for work-life balance such as Scandinavia, burnout has become an epidemic that organizations can no longer afford to ignore. For example, in Sweden, stress-related illness is now the fastest growing cause of long-term sick leave in the workplace.[60]

Like so many other high-performing professionals worldwide, I had internalized the idea that being overwhelmed was a personal failure and something I could fix myself with better time management, with productivity tools and with resilience. To do so, I downloaded productivity apps, I bought a new planner, watched productivity mindset videos on YouTube and I tried to meditate. But all my attempts failed as I couldn't out-plan the exhaustion. So I kept telling myself to keep going, *"just one more push"* and moved the end goal again and again.

Dr. Gabor Maté, in his book *The Myth of Normal*, explains that high-functioning and trauma-adapted individuals often suppress their needs until their health begins to break down.[61] The very traits that make someone reliable, competent and successful can also make them prone to ignoring warning signs. The more we are praised for being self-sufficient, the less permission we give ourselves to pause.

In my case, the signs were subtle at first. I started to get sick more often, my anxiety spiked and I stopped enjoying life at work and outside of it. And yet, I was still performing, I was still showing up and I was still being praised. It's so easy to miss burnout when you're being rewarded for it.

Christina Maslach's insight is simple but profound: burnout is not about too much work, but about insufficient recovery.[49] When recovery disappears, the system eventually falters. And the people most at risk are often the ones who care deeply. Introverts, neurodivergent professionals, women, people with impostor syndrome and anyone who already feels slightly outside the dominant mold. When you are used to proving yourself twice as hard, slowing down can feel like confirming every doubt.

The cost of caring too much is deep and with important consequences. Burnout doesn't make professionals better, it numbs them. It makes people become more quiet, more compliant, less creative and less present. It hollows out passion until the people who once drove the culture forward are reduced to shells of themselves. And yet, we continue to treat burnout as an individual weakness instead of a systemic failure. We send people to time management training instead of redesigning workloads and we offer subscriptions to wellness apps instead of changing expectations. And yet, in the middle of all this damage, we continue to celebrate endurance instead of creating the conditions for recovery.

What makes this even more paradoxical is how often corporate culture borrows language from sport. We speak about pushing through, playing to win, training harder, giving one hundred percent, controlling how we play. We celebrate high performance and resilience. And yet in sport, recovery is not optional. No serious athlete trains at maximum intensity every day. Rest days are programmed, sleep is protected and recovery is measured. Coaches understand that performance improves not during exertion, but during recovery. Muscles rebuild when they're allowed to rest. Endurance increases when stress is followed by restoration. In sport, overtraining without recovery leads to injury. In corporate life, we use the language of performance but discard the science of recovery. We admire the metaphor and ignore the physiology.

The truth is that none of us were ever meant to run on empty. Rest isn't an indulgence or a reward, it's necessary and it's maintenance. It's the precondition for clarity, creativity and leadership. And without it, nothing we build can last.

Tips and Tools: How to Lead Without Burning Out

Burnout isn't a personal flaw to be managed privately. It's a signal that the pace and expectations around us need to be examined. And while you may not control the entire system, you do shape the norms of your own work and, if you lead others, the norms of your team. Small shifts in how you define success, set boundaries and protect recovery can quietly interrupt a culture that equates depletion with dedication.

1. Redefine Success

In many corporate environments, busyness has quietly become a proxy for value. Being fully booked means you are important, a crowded calendar means your work is relevant and back-to-back meetings means you are in demand. If you reply late to emails, you're dedicated, if you are constantly available, you're committed. And before anyone really notices, those signals start to define what's valued.

But activity isn't the same as impact and exhaustion isn't evidence of effectiveness.

If success is defined primarily by output, speed and visibility, recovery will always feel uncomfortable. You might say that rest matters, you might even encourage your team to take breaks, but emotionally, slowing down can feel risky. And it can be so because when your value is tied to how much you produce, any pause starts to feel like a threat.

Redefining success isn't about lowering standards. it's about changing what the standard measures.

It means shifting from volume to contribution, from responsiveness to clarity, from endurance to sustainability. It means recognizing that discernment is often more valuable than availability, and that thoughtful restraint can create more progress than relentless motion.

Instead of asking how much you did this week, ask what genuinely moved forward. Instead of celebrating the person who stayed online the longest, pay attention to the one who solved something well and still had energy left. Instead of praising the fastest response, consider whether the response created an understanding that will last.

This isn't a cosmetic language shift, it's a recalibration of what gets rewarded. And what gets rewarded quietly becomes culture.

Burnout begins to weaken the moment intensity stops being the primary measure of worth.

In order to redefine success, here are some questions to reflect on:

- If someone looked at your calendar without context, what would they assume you value most?
- When did being tired start to feel like proof that you had done enough?
- If your team mirrored your current pace for the next five years, what would quietly become normal?
- What would success look like if sustainability wasn't optional, but required?
- If your sense of worth wasn't tied to output, how would you describe a genuinely good week?
- What behaviors are you reinforcing through what you praise and reward?
- What pace of work would you feel proud to sustain, not just this year, but over a decade?

When you begin measuring impact instead of intensity, clarity instead of speed, sustainability instead of stamina, something subtle shifts. The signal changes and over time, that signal does more to prevent burnout than any wellness initiative ever could.

2. Build Recovery Into the System

Most people don't burn out because they lack discipline, they burn out because recovery gets treated like something optional, something that happens if there's time left over at the end of the day.

In many corporate environments, recovery simply isn't built into the rhythm of work. Meetings run back to back without pause, conversations bleed into each other and evenings slowly fill with what you didn't get finished earlier. What was meant to be a temporary stretch quietly turns into a permanent pace.

And part of that rhythm isn't accidental, it comes from an older model of work. The industrial era was structured around shifts and physical separation. You worked your hours, you left the factory floor and, at least in theory, the day was done. The system assumed a clear stop. Recovery was built into the physical boundary between workplace and home. Modern office work removed that boundary. We carry our work in our pockets, in our inboxes and in our heads. The expectation of output stayed the same, but the structural stop disappeared. And when there's no clear stop, recovery doesn't just happen on its own, it has to be created deliberately.

Burnout is what happens when stress keeps accumulating and nothing interrupts it. Restoration doesn't occur by accident in an always-on environment, it needs structure.

Building recovery into the system starts with accepting something simple but uncomfortable. Human performance moves in cycles. Energy rises and falls, attention shifts and decision quality drops when we stay activated for too long. Sustainable leadership doesn't pretend those limits don't exist, it works with them.

Sometimes that looks very practical. Leaving space between meetings so you can reset before the next conversation, reducing constant context switching instead of trying to become faster at it or treating sleep as something that protects your professionalism, not something that competes with it. Because the quality of your thinking tomorrow depends on the recovery you allow today.

Recovery isn't laziness, it's maintenance.

We understand this instinctively in sport. No serious athlete trains at full intensity every day. Stress is followed by rest because improvements happen in recovery. Muscles rebuild in pause, endurance increases when effort is followed by restoration. The same is true for cognitive and emotional work. Insights often show up after distance, clarity appears when there's space and patience returns when the nervous system isn't constantly on alert.

When professionals build recovery into their rhythm, they're not signalling a lack of ambition, they're modeling sustainability. They're showing that performance doesn't require depletion and that stepping back is part of excellence, not a departure from it. And over time, that modeling shifts expectations far more quietly and effectively than any formal policy ever could.

Building recovery into the system doesn't require a dramatic overhaul, it starts with small structural choices. To help you make these small changes, here are some questions you can ask yourself:

- When during my day do I actually pause?
- Do I leave even five minutes between meetings, or do I book myself back to back all day?
- When was the last time I ended my day without checking one more thing?
- Am I sleeping enough to think clearly, or am I telling myself I'll catch up later?
- What part of my week feels most draining, and what would make it slightly lighter?
- If I removed just one source of constant interruption, what would it be?

Recovery only becomes culture when it's visible and consistent. And when recovery is designed rather than assumed, burnout starts to lose its grip.

3. Audit Your Energy, Not Just Your Calendar

Most leaders look at their calendar and think about time. How to fit more in, how to optimize it, how to make it efficient. But burnout rarely comes from a lack of hours, it comes from the quiet accumulation of energy drain that no one is paying attention to.

Two meetings can both take an hour, and on paper they look identical. But one might leave you clear, focused and steady, while the other leaves you foggy, slightly irritated and already behind before the next conversation begins. If you're only tracking time, you'll miss that difference. And over weeks and months, that difference adds up.

Auditing your energy means noticing what your day actually does to you. Not in a dramatic way, just honestly. Which conversations sharpen you and which ones exhaust you. Which tasks feel aligned with how you think and lead, and which ones require you to perform in ways that slowly wear you down.

It's also about patterns. Are you most drained after reactive status meetings? After conflicts you didn't have space to process? After constant context switching between topics that never quite finish? Or after moments where you had to mask more than you'd like to admit?

Energy isn't just about being introverted or extroverted, it's about alignment. The more your workday requires you to operate out of sync with how you actually think and function best, the more expensive it becomes. And if you don't consciously look at that cost, you'll simply assume exhaustion is normal.

Leaders and professionals at large often have more room to redesign than they think. Some meetings can be shorter, some updates don't need to be meetings at all, some decisions can wait until you're clearer rather than being made in a rushed state. But you can't redesign and change how you work before you have taken the time to examine and understand how you work.

So start by observing without judging and do it for a week or two by only observing and noticing your work and your energy. Pay attention to when you feel sharper at the end of something and when you feel depleted. Notice what lingers in your body long after the meeting ends. Notice when you feel stretched in a healthy way and when you feel slowly worn down.

To help you audit your energy, you can use the followings questions:

- Which parts of my day or week leave me clearer than when I started, and which parts leave me drained?
- Where do I feel most like myself at work, and where do I feel like I'm performing?
- What recurring commitment costs more energy than it creates?
- What could I shorten, delegate or redesign without anyone's performance suffering?
- If I removed just one unnecessary drain from my week, what would it be?

When you begin paying attention to energy instead of just time, you start working with sustainability in mind. And that shift is often the difference between staying effective for years and slowly turning work life into endurance.

4. Guard Your Cognitive Clarity

Burnout doesn't only show up as exhaustion, it also shows up as mental noise. You start reacting faster but thinking less deeply, you answer quickly, but you're not always sure you've considered the long-term implications. Everything feels urgent, and when everything feels urgent, understanding and depth quietly disappear.

Leadership isn't just about output, it's about judgment. It's about being able to hold ambiguity without rushing to closure, to tolerate uncertainty without panicking into action and to make decisions that won't need to be undone next week.

But clarity requires space.

If your days are packed with constant input, notifications, meetings and reactive decisions, your brain never gets the distance it needs to think well. You might still be performing, you might still be delivering, but the depth of your thinking begins to narrow. And that narrowing is subtle and it rarely feels dramatic. It just feels like you're slightly more impatient, slightly less curious and slightly quicker to move on.

Guarding your cognitive clarity means treating thinking time as part of the work, not as something you squeeze in if you're lucky. It means recognizing that reflection isn't a luxury, it's what prevents poor decisions disguised as efficiency.

Sometimes that looks like protecting a block of time where you're not available for quick chats. Sometimes it's postponing a decision until you've had a chance to think rather than responding in the moment just to clear it. Sometimes it's allowing silence in a conversation instead of filling it.

Clarity isn't created in constant motion, it's created in space.

To help you audit how well you're protecting your cognitive clarity, you can use the following questions:

- When was the last time I made an important decision without feeling rushed?
- Am I responding quickly because it's needed, or because I'm uncomfortable with silence?

- Where in my week do I actually have time to think?
- Have I recently postponed a decision to allow better thinking, or do I default to speed?
- What conversations would improve if I allowed more pause instead of immediate answers?
- If I continue operating at this pace, will my decisions get sharper or just faster?

Protecting your clarity isn't about doing less. It's about thinking better. And thinking better is one of the most sustainable forms of leadership you can model.

5. Stop Glorifying Urgency

One of the quiet drivers of burnout isn't workload alone, it's the constant sense that everything is urgent. Corporate cultures run on adrenaline. Emails are marked high priority, messages come with "quick question" or *"just need this fast."* Deadlines tighten without discussion and slowly, urgency becomes the default tone.

The problem is that urgency feels productive. It creates momentum and it gives the illusion of importance. When something is urgent, it feels significant. But when everything is urgent, we lose our sense of what actually matters and we stop asking what truly matters and start reacting to whatever is loudest.

Over time, this constant activation rewires how teams operate. People rush not because the situation demands it, but because rushing has become normal. They respond quickly, even when the quality of the response would improve with thought. They escalate small issues because escalation feels safer than delay and leaders, often unintentionally, reinforce the pattern by praising speed over clarity.

There's a difference between something being important and something being urgent. Important work often requires depth, reflection and sequencing. Urgent work demands immediate action. When we start blurring the line between the two, everything gets treated as both, and exhaustion follows.

Stopping the glorification of urgency doesn't mean ignoring deadlines or lowering standards, it means being deliberate about when speed is truly required and when it's simply a habit. It means noticing when adrenaline is driving decisions more than intention.

To help you examine how urgency operates in your work life, you can use the following questions:

- Is this actually urgent, or does it just feel urgent?
- What would happen if this waited until tomorrow or until next week?
- Am I escalating this because it matters, or because I'm uncomfortable with delay?
- Where have I rewarded speed when I should have rewarded thoughtfulness?
- What tone do my messages set, calm and deliberate, or pressured and reactive?
- Am I creating fake deadlines simply to keep momentum?
- If my team experienced fewer artificial emergencies, how would their energy change?

Leaders set emotional pace as much as operational pace. When you slow the tone, clarify priorities and resist unnecessary escalation, you don't just reduce stress, you create room for better thinking.

And over time, that shift from constant urgency to deliberate action does more to prevent burnout than any resilience workshop ever could.

Visual Summary

Practice	What It Looks Like	Why It Works
1. Redefine Success	You measure impact instead of busyness. You reward clarity, contribution and sustainable pace rather than visible exhaustion.	When intensity stops being the main signal of value, burnout loses its cultural status. What gets rewarded becomes the norm.
2. Build Recovery Into the System	You design pauses into your rhythm. You leave space between meetings, protect sleep and create real stopping points instead of hoping recovery happens later.	Performance improves through restoration. When recovery is structural, strain doesn't silently accumulate.
3. Audit Your Energy, Not Just Your Calendar	You pay attention to what sharpens you and what drains you. You redesign recurring energy leaks before they become normal.	Burnout builds gradually. Energy awareness exposes hidden depletion before it turns into exhaustion.
4. Guard Your Cognitive Clarity	You protect thinking time, allow pause before decisions and reduce unnecessary context switching.	Clear judgment requires space. Without it, decisions become faster but weaker.
5. Stop Glorifying Urgency	You separate important from immediate work. You question artificial deadlines and model calm instead of adrenaline.	When everything feels urgent, clarity disappears. Slowing the emotional pace protects both performance and culture.

Micro-Practice: Remove One Signal of Exhaustion

Burnout rarely begins with one big decision, it builds through hundreds of small moments where urgency is assumed and rest is postponed. Many of us don't choose to overwork consciously, we simply react.

For the next week, choose one small behavior that quietly signals that exhaustion equals commitment, and stop doing it. Not everything, just one.

It might be replying to emails late at night even though it could wait.

It might be booking yourself back to back without transition.

It might be saying yes immediately instead of pausing.

Don't make it a declaration, just do it quietly as a signal to yourself and to others.

Then observe what happens.

Does anything actually fall apart?

Does performance suffer?

Or do things continue more or less as before, only slightly steadier?

Burnout culture isn't maintained by dramatic decisions, it's maintained by small repeated signals about what is valued. Change one signal and you begin to test whether exhaustion is truly required or simply assumed.

Practical Quick Phrases

When exhaustion becomes normalized, it can be hard to find the words to slow things down without feeling like you're letting someone down. Many of us freeze in the moment, not because we don't know our limits, but because we don't want to appear uncommitted or difficult. These phrases aren't scripts and they're not meant to be used all at once. They're simple, neutral language you can lean on when urgency shows up and you need a way to protect your energy without over-explaining or apologizing.

- *"I'd like to think this through before responding."*
- *"Let's separate what's important from what's immediate."*
- *"I can look at this tomorrow when I'm clearer."*
- *"What happens if we give this 24 hours?"*
- *"Can we prioritize before we react?"*
- *"This matters, but it doesn't need to be decided right now."*
- *"Let's be clear on what actually needs to happen today."*
- *"I'm at capacity today, let's schedule this properly."*

Checklist: What Will You Try This Week?

Burnout culture doesn't shift because we understand it, it shifts because we change small behaviors that quietly reinforce it. The actions below aren't dramatic and they don't require a full redesign of your workload. They're small adjustments you can make this week to protect your energy and model a more sustainable pace.

- Question one moment where urgency feels automatic.
- Let one non-critical request wait until the next working day.
- Leave space between two meetings.
- Protect one small window for recovery without explaining it.
- Notice when exhaustion is subtly praised or treated as commitment.

Closing: Rest Is Not Laziness, It's Leadership

I used to believe that value was proven through relentless output and that rest was something you earned later on, when you're done and have emptied yourself completely. If I was tired, it meant I cared, if I was stretched thin, it meant I was committed. So I pushed through, I overdelivered and I wore exhaustion as quiet proof that I belonged.

But I was wrong.

Burnout isn't strength, it's what happens when you've ignored your own limits for too long and convinced yourself that doing more is the only way to secure your place. You can still be praised while it's happening, you can still be promoted and you can still look stable from the outside. And that's what makes it so deceptive, because the erosion isn't always visible at first. It happens gradually. It happens when clarity is slowly lost, when patience starts to shorten and when the body is constantly tense even when you tell yourself you're fine.

I remember a department gathering years ago where I showed up completely depleted. I was presenting and facilitating exercises, trying to be steady and inspiring because that's what I believed professionalism and leadership required. On the surface I probably looked composed. My voice was calm, my slides were prepared and people told me afterwards that I'd done well. But inside I felt numb. I wasn't leading from energy, I was leading from endurance. And it took me years to understand that performing stability isn't the same as living it, and that the effort of holding that performance together was quietly costing me my clarity, my connection to others and eventually my health.

It took time to see this clearly, and the pattern isn't unique.

Even governments have recognized that constant availability isn't sustainable. In 2017, France introduced what's known as the *"right to disconnect,"* acknowledging that employees shouldn't be expected to respond to emails and messages outside working hours. It wasn't framed as laziness, it was framed as protection. Because when recovery disappears, the cost doesn't stay personal, it becomes societal. And the fact that legislation was required says something about how deeply overwork has become normalized.[62,63]

There's a phrase people sometimes say, half-jokingly and half-proudly, *"I'll rest when I'm dead."* It's usually delivered as if endurance were admirable and exhaustion were the price of seriousness. But if you live by that logic long enough, what slowly disappears isn't your ambition, it's your capacity. You don't just postpone rest, you postpone clarity, presence and the steadiness that leadership actually depends on.

Leadership built on burnout can look impressive for a while. It can even deliver results in the short term, but over time it becomes brittle. When leaders are depleted, teams absorb that depletion. When leaders never stop, teams don't feel they're allowed to stop either. And when recovery is treated as indulgence, performance slowly turns into pressure that no one quite knows how to step out of.

Rest isn't a break from being professional or from leading, it's part of it. It protects judgment, steadies emotion and restores perspective. It creates the distance you need to think well and the space you need to respond instead of simply reacting. And perhaps most importantly, it models something your team is watching closely, whether they say it or not: that sustainability isn't weakness, it's wisdom.

If we want to model resilience, we have to model restoration. If we want to lead high-performing teams, we have to create cultures where energy is protected rather than quietly extracted. And if we want to last in our careers, not just survive them, we have to stop proving ourselves by how much we can endure and start proving ourselves by how intentionally we pace.

You're not a machine designed for constant output and your value isn't measured in hours logged or inboxes cleared. Your capacity to work and lead is shaped by the clarity you maintain, the steadiness you bring into difficult rooms and the discipline you show in protecting what allows you to keep showing up fully over time.

Rest isn't laziness and it isn't indulgence. It's not something you earn after proving how much you can endure. It's part of how you stay clear enough to make good decisions, calm enough to hold difficult conversations and human enough to remain connected to the people you lead.

And when recovery becomes part of how you work or lead, you're no longer proving how much you can endure, you're protecting how long you can remain effective.

Rule 7: Grieve and Lead at the Same Time

"Grief is in two parts. The first is loss. The second is the remaking of life."
Anne Roiphe

When I lost my friend Theresa, I didn't know how to function professionally, and even less how to lead my team while grieving. She was my best friend, my colleague, my professional confidante, my anchor. She was the one who always knew when something was off and she could decode my silence better than most people could interpret words. Her death was sudden and with it I found myself in a territory I recognized but wasn't prepared to enter again. Eleven years earlier, at the beginning of my professional career, I lost my mother without warning. Now, with Theresa's passing, I was once again facing grief while trying to keep working, while having to show up and while having a team to lead.

At the same time, I was in the middle of a divorce. Another ending, another loss. I was grieving both at once, and still going to work every day, expected to function, decide, and lead as if nothing fundamental had shifted.

This experience isn't unique to me. We all lose people we love, and the world still expects us to log on, perform, and carry on. Our calendars don't care, the deadlines still exist, meetings continue to be booked and people continue to need direction. While most of us will take a few days off to absorb the initial shock, grief doesn't resolve itself in a matter of days. We return to work still heavy with loss, still in pain and we do our best to put on a smile when we can.

In my case, after a few days off, I went back to work. I kept showing up, but I wasn't there. I moved through my days in a fog, managing logistics and to dos while feeling numb inside. I remember sitting in a leadership meeting nodding along while internally screaming *"None of this matters! We're discussing marketing issues... who cares!"*

Of course, people were kind at first. They asked me how I was on my first day back, but after that, no one asked if I was ok. I didn't offer to share how I felt either. Masking grief felt like an unspoken expectation, something I did to avoid making others uncomfortable at work. Because grief does make people uncomfortable, especially at work. So I masked and grieved silently during work hours, I continued to lead my team and it exhausted me. It was only later that I realized this silent exhaustion had been named before.

After her husband's sudden death in 2015, Sheryl Sandberg, then Chief Operating Officer at Facebook, returned to work within weeks. Not because she was untouched by what had happened, but because work provided structure at a time when everything else felt fractured. In *Option B*, she reflects on the tension between functioning and falling apart, and how rebuilding a life after loss is not about suppressing grief but learning to live alongside it. She describes how restoring meaning required showing up for others, yet she could not do that honestly until she first allowed herself to fully experience the devastation. Grief was not something to power through, it was something to acknowledge, endure, and gradually weave into a remade life.[64]

Sheryl led through her grief, not by pretending it didn't exist, but by learning to carry it differently. Her vulnerability sparked a much-needed conversation in Silicon Valley and beyond about the realities of loss at work. What her story revealed was not exceptional strength, but a shared reality: returning to work does not mean grief has ended. It only means we are expected to carry it quietly.

The problem is that most companies aren't built to hold grief. We're given a few days off, then expected to return, perform, and lead as if loss follows a schedule. But grief doesn't respect calendar invites or meeting agendas. It doesn't pause during work hours or soften because you're meant to give feedback or make decisions. It shows up when it does, often quietly and unexpectedly, while you're trying to look composed and professional.

Grief expert David Kessler, who coauthored *On Grief and Grieving* with Elisabeth Kübler-Ross, argues that grief is not something to fix or resolve as if it were a technical problem. It is something we learn to carry, something that reshapes us and stays with us as part of our ongoing story.[65]

This is where leadership becomes complicated. Most leaders are never taught how to lead through grief. At least, I've not seen any leadership manuals with a chapter called *"Grieve and Lead"*. We're taught to stay strong, to keep things moving and to protect performance and momentum. We're taught to minimize disruption even when what we're carrying is anything but small. In the absence of language, space or permission, many of us default to silence and endurance, setting a tone of professionalism that quietly asks people to leave their humanity at the door.

But what if the tone we set is one of humanity?

Grief Is Not a Detour from Leadership, It's Part of the Path

We are not machines, even if corporate systems sometimes behave as though we're expected to function like them. Work culture often assumes that we can compartmentalize our humanity and leave it out at the office door and step into meetings untouched by what is happening in our personal lives. Grief makes it clear that the separation between personal and professional life was always an illusion.

Grief is not a temporary productivity glitch that can be solved with a few days off. It's a full body and mind experience that reshapes attention, energy, memory and regulation. It can be triggered by death, but also by divorce, illness, miscarriage, estrangement, burnout, or the loss of a future you had quietly built your identity around. You don't need to lose a person to grieve, and grief doesn't operate according to business hours.

In *Finding Meaning: The Sixth Stage of Grief*, David Kessler describes grief as the continuation of love after loss.[66] When that love has nowhere to go, it doesn't disappear, it shifts form. It can surface as irritability, cognitive fog, fatigue, overcontrol or detachment that feels unfamiliar even to ourselves. In leadership roles, those shifts matter because they shape how we decide, how we listen and how we respond under pressure.

And yet many organizations still operate as if productivity is linear and emotion is an obstacle to overcome. The implicit expectation is that once someone has returned to work, they've also returned to full capacity. Research published in the Harvard Business Review highlights that emotionally intelligent leadership, particularly leadership grounded in empathy and self-awareness, strengthens trust and organizational effectiveness over time.[67] Trust and psychological safety do not emerge from pretending that loss doesn't exist, they grow when people experience that their humanity is not a liability.

In *Creativity, Inc.*, Ed Catmull reflects on leading Pixar through moments of personal loss and how those experiences challenged the idea that leaders should remain emotionally distant from their teams.[68] Rather than maintaining a polished façade, he chose to acknowledge the impact of grief and recognize that creative work doesn't happen in isolation from the human experience. By doing so, he reinforced a truth that many workplaces resist: personal and professional lives are never fully separate. At Pixar, this openness didn't weaken authority or compromise performance, it deepened trust and strengthened collaboration during demanding periods.

Grief also disrupts our internal systems in ways that are not always visible. It interferes with concentration, executive functioning and emotional regulation, and for leaders who are already carrying significant responsibility, that disruption can feel destabilizing. For neurodivergent leaders in particular, the impact can be amplified. Many rely on structure, predictability and carefully managed routines to function at a high level, and grief unsettles those foundations. When your processing is nonlinear to begin with, and when you already expend energy masking and monitoring your responses in professional spaces, grief adds another layer of demand to an already taxed system.

Because of this, grief doesn't always look like visible sadness. It can look like shutdown, sensory overload, decision paralysis or an uncharacteristic withdrawal from conversations you would normally lead with clarity. When the pressure to remain composed is layered on top of these internal shifts, many leaders move into survival mode, prioritizing performance over regulation and silence over honesty.

Grief doesn't disqualify you from leadership, it changes the conditions under which you lead. It asks for a different pace, a different level of awareness and a different kind of care, both for yourself and for others. When grief is acknowledged rather than suppressed, it doesn't weaken leadership, it deepens it.

Leadership in grief requires more than quiet endurance, it requires naming what is happening. It requires telling your team when your capacity has shifted, acknowledging when your headspace is limited and inviting others to speak up when you miss something. Silence may feel professional, but it reinforces the very culture of masking that makes grief harder to carry. When leaders speak about loss openly, they don't destabilize their teams, they create clarity about reality.

Leadership in grief is not about performing stoicism or suppressing emotion in the name of professionalism, it's about awareness, regulation and care. It's about knowing your limits, communicating them with integrity and choosing presence over perfection when your capacity has shifted.

The Myth of Either Or

I used to think I had to choose:

Show up OR fall apart.
Lead OR grieve.
Perform OR pause.

For a long time, I believed those things were mutually exclusive and that I had to choose between them. I believed that if I allowed myself to feel the grief fully, I would lose my grip on leadership and with it the credibility I had worked so hard to build. I feared that showing how shaken I was would quietly erode my authority, that people would start to question my judgment, my stability and my capacity to carry responsibility. I worried that I would disappoint those who relied on me, that I would become unreliable in their eyes and that the version of me they trusted would begin to fracture.

When Theresa died, I wasn't only grieving her, I was also in the middle of a divorce. Two endings unfolding at the same time, two ruptures demanding more energy than I felt I had. I was exhausted and unfocused, moving through days with brain fog and struggling to concentrate on tasks that would normally have been simple. And still, every morning, I went to work. I logged on, joined meetings, made decisions and led my team.

Taking sick leave could have been an option and no one would have questioned it. But I could not imagine staying home with nothing but the silence and the weight of it all surrounding me. I didn't want to sit alone bathing in my sorrow. As disorienting as work felt, it also gave me structure and it gave my days shape when everything else felt unstable. At times it was an escape, at other times it was simply something solid to hold onto. However I longed for a pause, there was no clear way to process one loss before the next one insisted on being felt, and work became both the place where I somewhat functioned and the place where I hid.

But hiding didn't mean the grief stayed contained and showing up didn't create a clean boundary between the part of me that was leading and the part of me that was grieving. Grief is not a clean before and after moment. It's not a chapter you close neatly so you can return to being productive and clear minded. It seeps into your calendar, your emails, your conversations. Some days it appears as forgetfulness, other days as tears behind closed doors. And sometimes it arrives as numbness, as if you are watching yourself from a distance performing the role of a leader while part of you is somewhere else entirely. This is not detachment or indifference, but a form of dissociation, a protective response when the mind creates distance from what feels too heavy to hold all at once.

I remember days where I was managing deliverables and deadlines while my body felt hollow. Days where I was speaking in meetings while internally trying to hold myself together. I felt completely split, as if the person who was grieving and the person who was leading were two entirely different people occupying the same space.

But they weren't.

The real turning point wasn't when I returned to normal. In truth, eighteen months later, as I write this, I am still not sure I ever did. Grief doesn't restore you to who you were before, it reshapes you. I will never be the person I was before Theresa's passing and before my divorce.

The real shift came when I stopped trying to confine my grief to evenings and weekends. Not because I had reached some moment of clarity or wisdom, but because I no longer had the energy to keep masking at work. I couldn't continue pretending I was fine while everything inside me felt unstable. So I was honest with my team. I told them I was going through a lot, that I was not fully myself and that my headspace was limited. I asked them to tell me if I forgot things, to speak up if they needed me and I did not see it, and to let me know if I was missing something or falling short without realizing it. I was not asking to be excused, I was asking to be supported.

Naming my grief was not a weakness and speaking openly about my capacity didn't erode my credibility. It did the opposite. It allowed me to stop performing certainty and composure, and it made my leadership more honest. In doing so, it also gave others quiet permission to exhale, to be human and to acknowledge what they were carrying without fear that it would cost them their legitimacy at work.

As Megan Devine argues in her book *It's OK That You're Not OK*, grief is not a problem to be solved but an experience that needs to be witnessed.[69] This is true in life and it's true in leadership. When grief is acknowledged rather than avoided, people don't fall apart. Instead they settle, they breathe and they stay connected.

The problem is that most workplaces still struggle to make room for that kind of humanity. Strength is often defined as emotional containment, as the ability to carry on without showing what hurts. Leaders are praised for staying composed, for managing their emotions privately, for rising above pain rather than acknowledging it. But this expectation doesn't create healthy leadership, it creates a disconnect. When there's little room for vulnerability, people are left to navigate grief alone. We ask grieving employees when they'll be back at one hundred percent instead of asking what support would help them right now and in the coming weeks. And in that silence, grief becomes something to hide, rather than something that can be carried together.

Research published in *The Transdisciplinary Journal of Management* found that in the first month after the loss of a loved one, more than half of employees didn't feel capable of performing their job duties at their usual level.[70] In other words, many people are back at work while still struggling to function. And according to estimates frequently cited in workplace grief research, unresolved grief carries significant productivity costs for organizations each year.[71]

But beyond the statistics, there is a simpler truth: people don't stop being human because they have a job.

And here's the part I didn't expect, grieving has made me a better leader. Not louder and not tougher, but more tender. I'm more present and less reactive, more aware of my limits and the limits of others. But I'm also less intimidated. When you've walked through something that fractures your life and survived it, other people's titles, egos and manufactured urgency lose some of their weight. The things that once felt overwhelming or politically charged don't carry the same intensity anymore. I'm more grounded now, more certain of who I am and what I stand for. I trust my judgment more than I did before, and I'm clearer about what matters and more willing to question what does not. I don't confuse noise with importance the way I once did. I'm more comfortable holding my position without over explaining myself, and more willing to name what feels misaligned. I'm not any of those things because I was strong despite the grief, but because I was changed by it.

And in ways I didn't anticipate, the losses reshaped my courage. I'm not sure I would've dared to write this book if I hadn't gone through Theresa's death and my divorce. Grief stripped away some of the illusions I was still holding about safety and approval and forced me to confront what actually matters and what I'm willing to stand for.

We often admire leaders for their clarity, their resilience, their ability to keep going no matter what. But the leaders I trust most are the ones who have been cracked open by life and chose to keep showing up anyway, not with a polished façade or a perfect mask, but with honesty about what they carry.

You do not have to choose between grief and leadership. Either or is a myth. You can hold both.

Tips and Tools: Leading While Healing

1. Name It Instead of Numbing It

Grief becomes heavier when you pretend it isn't there. The effort of acting normal often drains more energy than the grief itself. When you refuse to acknowledge what you're carrying, it tends to surface indirectly through impatience, foggy thinking, overwork, or emotional withdrawal.

Naming grief does not require dramatic disclosure; it begins with honesty about your current state. Leadership during loss starts with alignment between what you are experiencing and how you are showing up.

You might begin privately by telling yourself:

- This is affecting me more than I want to admit.
- I'm not okay, even if I look fine.
- I don't have the same bandwidth I usually do.

Before a meeting, pause and ask yourself:

- What shape am I in today?
- How much do I actually have to give?
- Am I pushing because it matters, or because I don't want anyone to see I'm struggling?

If and when it feels appropriate, you can extend that honesty outward towards others:

- *"I'm going through something difficult, so my headspace may be more limited than usual."*
- *"My head is a bit scattered these days."*
- *"If I miss something, please tell me."*

This is not oversharing, it's context. It reduces confusion and prevents misinterpretation and it also models something rare in leadership: honesty about your capacity.

Numbing often looks like pushing harder, speaking more sharply, or disappearing into busyness. Naming, by contrast, is a stabilizing act. It allows you to lead from your actual capacity rather than from a performance of resilience.

You don't have to narrate or explain your grief in detail, but you do have to stop denying that it exists.

2. Recalibrate Expectations

Grief changes your capacity whether you admit it or not. Your focus narrows, your tolerance drops, your thinking slows in ways that can feel unfamiliar and frustrating. If you keep measuring yourself against who you were before the loss, you will constantly feel behind and that quiet pressure will drain you faster than the grief itself.

Recalibrating expectations is not about lowering standards. It's about being honest about what you can realistically carry right now. It means deciding, consciously, what actually needs your attention and what you are holding onto out of habit, fear or pride.

Instead of asking yourself how to keep up, try asking:

- What truly matters this week?
- What can wait, even if I do not like letting it wait?
- Where do I actually add value right now?

Grief can make everything feel urgent because your system is already stretched, but not everything that feels urgent deserves the same weight.

And this can't just be a private adjustment. If your capacity has shifted, the way you prioritize will shift too. That means being clear about what you are focusing on and what you are not. It means saying, without apology, *"This is what I can give right now,"* and trusting that clarity is more responsible than silent overextension.

When you lead others, this becomes even more important. Teams take their cues from how you show up. If you continue to push at full speed without acknowledging that your capacity has shifted, you may unintentionally create confusion or unrealistic expectations. Being clear about what you are prioritizing and what you are not doesn't lower the bar, it simply makes the bar visible.

Grief changes the conditions under which you lead. Recalibrating expectations is how you lead within those new conditions instead of pretending they don't exist.

3. Create a Grief-Safe Environment

Grief is a universal human experience. Almost everyone will face loss at some point during their working life, yet many workplaces act as if it doesn't exist. As a leader, you can shift that simply by naming grief as real and legitimate.

Creating a grief-safe environment doesn't mean lowering standards or suspending accountability. It means recognizing that people are whole human beings, not roles, and that performance fluctuates when someone's world has shifted. It also means removing the unspoken expectation that professionalism requires emotional neutrality.

A grief-safe environment is not built through policy alone, it's built through tone, through pacing and through what you acknowledge and what you ignore.

You can normalize compassion through small, direct language:

- *"You don't have to pretend you're fine."*
- *"We don't expect you to power through this."*
- *"I don't expect you to be at your best right now."*

You also normalize it through behavior. You adjust deadlines when possible, you reduce unnecessary pressure, you check in more than once, not only on day one and you avoid turning someone's pain into silence because it feels uncomfortable.

When someone returns to work after a loss, don't assume they're back at full capacity. Ask: *"What kind of support would help you most right now?"* And be prepared to listen without immediately trying to solve.

You can't fix anyone's grief, but you can remove the pressure to hide it.

4. Build in Buffer Zones

Grief is unpredictable. You may wake up steady and unravel by midday. Something small can hit unexpectedly and throw off your concentration, your patience or your energy. If your schedule leaves no room to absorb that, the day becomes survival rather than leadership.

Building buffer zones into your calendar is not an indulgence, it's protective and it creates space to regulate instead of react.

That might mean blocking fifteen minutes between meetings, even if it results in fewer calls. When you're carrying loss, transitions require more energy than usual. Without pauses, the strain accumulates quietly and builds as the day goes on.

It might mean declining optional meetings with a simple, *"I won't be able to join, thank you for understanding."* You don't owe anyone an explanation for protecting your capacity.

It might mean stepping outside once a day, even briefly, without your phone. Not to optimize anything, just to pause. When you move from meeting to meeting without a break, everything blurs together and your tolerance drops without you noticing. A few minutes of space can stop the day from turning into one long reaction.

Buffer zones are not about doing less, they're about creating enough space to lead without running on fumes.

5. Ask for (and Accept) Help

Grief exposes your limits whether you like it or not. The illusion that you can carry everything alone becomes harder to maintain, especially when your energy is already reduced.

Many leaders struggle here. We're used to being the one who absorbs pressure, who solves problems, who doesn't need much. Admitting that you can't hold everything can feel uncomfortable, even threatening. But pretending you can only increases the strain.

Asking for help doesn't mean collapsing, it simply means being realistic.

You can say:

- *"I can't take this on right now."*
- *"I'm going to need support on this."*
- *"Can you handle this piece?"*

That is not weakness, it's clarity.

And when someone offers help, accept it without turning it into a performance of independence. Say, "Yes, thank you," and leave it there. You don't need to explain why you deserve support.

Look at your responsibilities with honesty and ask yourself:

- *What am I still trying to carry out of habit?*
- *What would actually happen if I let this go?*
- *Where am I holding on because it protects my identity, not because it's necessary?*

If someone on your team is grieving, be specific when you check-in on them. *"Let me know if you need anything"* sounds kind but requires them to do the emotional labor of asking. Take it one step further and say something like, *"I'll take this off your plate,"* or *"You don't need to handle this right now."*

Leadership is not about proving you can endure everything alone, it's about knowing when shared load is the wiser choice.

Visual Summary

Practice	What It Looks Like	Why It Works
1. Name It Instead of Numbing It	Acknowledging what you're carrying privately or out loud instead of pretending nothing has changed.	Naming reality reduces internal pressure and prevents it from leaking out as impatience, exhaustion or withdrawal.
2. Recalibrate Expectations	Being clear about reduced capacity, narrowing focus, and prioritizing what actually matters right now.	Clear priorities protect energy, improve decision quality and prevent silent overextension.
3. Create a Grief-Safe Environment	Using direct language, adjusting pressure where possible, and acknowledging loss instead of avoiding it.	When grief isn't hidden, people conserve energy and stay connected instead of masking or withdrawing.
4. Build in Buffer Zones	Fewer meetings, intentional pauses, and space between interactions.	Pauses interrupt accumulation of pressure and help you respond instead of react.
5. Ask for and Accept Help	Delegating honestly, saying yes to support, and offering specific help to others.	Shared load reduces isolation and makes leadership more sustainable during loss.

Micro-Practice: A Two-Minute Reset

Grief feels overwhelming because it is not something you can solve. When the pain is this large, trying to push through it usually makes it heavier. What helps is not a breakthrough moment, but small anchors that bring you back into the present.

This practice is for those moments during the workday when grief rises unexpectedly and you need to steady yourself without shutting down.

Try this:

1. Set a timer for two minutes.
2. Close your eyes if you can, or soften your gaze. Breathe slowly in and out.
3. Ask yourself, quietly: *"What do I need right now?"*
4. Do one small thing toward that need. Sip water. Stretch your body. Cancel or delay a meeting. Step outside for fresh air. Message someone you trust.

You're not trying to fix anything, you're creating just enough stability to stay present.

Two minutes won't erase grief, but it can interrupt the spiral. And sometimes that's enough to return to the room without pretending you were never affected.

Practical Quick Phrases

When you're grieving, finding words can take more effort than usual. You may know you need to say something, but you might not have the energy to find the right words. The sentences below are simple and direct, and they can help when your capacity shifts and you need language that is honest without being dramatic.

When you're leading or working while grieving:

- *"I'm dealing with a personal loss, so I may move a bit more slowly right now."*
- *"I'm here, even if I'm not at my best today."*
- *"I don't have full capacity for this right now. Let's focus on what actually matters."*
- *"Some days are heavier than others. Today's one of them."*

- *"I'm not looking for solutions. I just wanted to name what I'm carrying."*
- *"If I seem quieter than usual, that's why."*
- *"Can we revisit this when I have more clarity?"*
- *"I appreciate your patience. It helps."*

When you're supporting others:

- *"You don't have to pretend you're fine here."*
- *"What would feel supportive right now?"*
- *"We can adjust. You don't have to push through."*
- *"I'm glad you told me."*

These phrases aren't about lowering standards, they're about removing confusion. Clear language prevents misinterpretation and makes space for reality without turning grief into the center of everything.

Checklist: What Will You Try This Week?

If you're going through loss right now, choose one small action to try this week.

- I'll have an honest conversation with my manager about where I need flexibility.
- I'll decline one unnecessary meeting and use that time to reset.
- I'll ask for support instead of waiting until I'm overwhelmed.
- I'll acknowledge grief, mine or someone else's, instead of pretending it isn't there.
- I'll return to this chapter when I forget that I'm allowed to grieve and lead at the same time.

Closing: There's No Playbook for Grief (But There Is Permission)

I was supposed to be in London three days after Theresa passed away. I had bought tickets months earlier for the final European show of the Eras Tour. It was one of the few things I had genuinely been looking forward to during the worst part of my divorce. At that time, joy was rare.

Five days before the show, Theresa died. I had planned to take time off for the trip, but I hadn't planned to grieve while traveling. And yet that's what it became. I didn't go to celebrate, I went because I couldn't sit still with the pain. I needed distance from the divorce, from the loss, from the collapse of everything familiar. I needed a few hours where the world wasn't mine to manage. Something magical and unapologetically alive. Music, lights, girlhood and thousands of voices singing together. A different atmosphere, a different emotional frequency and a space where I could feel something other than collapse.

When I came back, nothing had resolved itself but time had moved. I was still a parent, still in the middle of a divorce, still a leader. I still had to make decisions and I was still someone others looked to for clarity.

But I had changed.

No one tells you how to lead after this kind of change. The advice is thin: take time off, be professional, take care of yourself. But grief isn't linear. Some days you can focus and lead with presence, other days the thought of small talk by the coffee machine feels impossible. And both can be true at the same time.

Writers and public figures have named this reality before. In *Notes on Grief*, Chimamanda Ngozi Adichie describes how loss alters the texture of time itself and how even functioning can feel strange and at times disloyal to the loss. And yet, she returned to writing, speaking and leading. Not despite the grief, but with it woven into who she had become.[72]

Reading others' reflections on grief helped me. Not because they offered a formula, but because they confirmed something essential: there isn't a correct way to lead while grieving. There is only the choice to do it honestly.

Psychologist George Bonanno, who has studied grief for decades, argues that resilience is not the absence of grief, but the capacity to adapt while experiencing it. And leadership, real leadership, is the ability to navigate life as it actually is, not as we wish it would be.[73]

After a couple of weeks of trying to remain composed at work, I did the one thing that mattered most. I stopped performing and told my team the truth. Not in detail, not dramatically, just plainly. I let them see that my capacity had shifted. At the time it felt extremely risky, but it was real and I needed to give myself permission to not be who I was before.

And in doing so, I learned that my team didn't need me to be invincible, they needed me to be human.

You can lead with grieving.

You can feel hollow and still be honest

You can take space and still carry responsibility.

The real work isn't hiding the pain, it's choosing honesty over performance, even when it feels vulnerable.

And that may be the most courageous form of leadership there is.

Conclusion to Part 2: How We Lead

Leadership is often described in idealized terms: vision, charisma, authority, confidence. But real leadership, when we take the time to think about it, rarely looks like that. In practice, leadership is built in the quiet and repeated choices we make every day. It also takes shape in the moments of uncertainty, in how we respond under pressure and in how we treat our energy, our limits and the people who depend on us.

Part 2 of this book has not been about becoming a different kind of leader, it has been about learning how to lead without abandoning yourself and about unlearning the habits that have made leadership unsustainable for far too many people.

Across these chapters, a different picture of leadership has emerged: one that's less about performance and more about presence. This different picture of leadership is less about pushing through and more about paying attention. It's less about control, but more about responsibility.

Rule 4 was about accepting uncertainty and letting go of the belief that good leadership means having all the answers. In many corporate environments, leadership is still associated with certainty, speed and confidence. The person who speaks first and sounds most sure is often seen as the strongest in the room. But meaningful leadership rarely comes from certainty. It comes from the courage to not know, from curiosity, from listening without rushing to fix, and from resisting the urge to perform competence. When leaders shift from protecting their authority to asking better questions, they create space for others to think, contribute and challenge. That's how trust is built and how teams become safer, smarter and more engaged.

Rule 5 reframed boundaries as cultural signals rather than personal preferences. Boundaries are never neutral. Leaders teach others what's acceptable through what they model, tolerate and reward. When leaders work late in silence, skip breaks or remain permanently available, they don't just manage their own workload, they quietly set the standard for everyone watching. Exhaustion then becomes normalized and constant availability becomes expected. But boundaries aren't about rigidity or control, they're about alignment and they show what truly matters. When leaders protect their time, energy and health, and communicate their limits clearly, they give others permission to do the same. Over time, that shapes culture far more powerfully than any policy. And that matters because the culture we create decides whether people thrive in leadership or quietly burn out inside it.

Rule 6 challenged one of the most persistent myths in leadership culture: that depletion is the price of ambition and burnout is proof of commitment. In many organizations, being constantly busy and stretched isn't just common, it's admired. Exhaustion becomes a badge of honor and recovery is quietly downplayed, as if rest signals a lack of drive. But burnout isn't strength, it's a signal that demands have exceeded capacity for too long. And burnout never stays contained. When leaders are depleted, teams feel it through urgency, reactivity and instability. Sustainable leadership isn't indulgent or soft, it's responsible. Protecting energy, rest and recovery isn't about caring less, it's about ensuring you can and your team can still deliver tomorrow.

Rule 7 confronted one of the hardest truths of leadership: life doesn't pause because we have responsibilities. Grief, loss, illness and personal crises don't wait until they're professionally convenient. Many leaders believe they must compartmentalize their pain to remain credible. So they mask it, carry it alone and try to lead as if nothing has changed. But grief doesn't disappear when it's ignored. It shows up in our focus, our energy, our judgment and our ability to connect. Leading through grief isn't unprofessional, it's inevitable over the course of a lifetime. And when leaders acknowledge what they're carrying instead of hiding it, they don't weaken their authority, they deepen trust and make leadership more human, honest and sustainable.

Taken together, these four rules point to a quieter, more resilient form of leadership and to a way to lead I believe is needed across all organizations. The old model where being a leader means to be tough and strong is outdated and changes are needed to lead the current and future generations. This new and more sustainable leadership doesn't rely on constant performance, it doesn't demand self-abandonment, and doesn't require pretending that life isn't happening outside of work. This needed leadership makes room for energy, for limits, and for truth.

How we lead isn't only measured in outcomes and results, it's felt in the tone we set, the cultures we shape, and the permission we give others to be human. Leadership lives in the questions we ask, the boundaries we honor, and the care we extend to ourselves and to others.

Part 2 has been about learning how to lead without erasing yourself in the process. It's been about choosing presence over performance, about sustainability over sacrifice and most importantly about reality over illusion.

And once we begin lead this way, a different question emerges:

What happens when leadership itself starts to change?

That question is where Part 3 begins.

PART 3 – CHANGING THE GAME

"You never change things by fighting the existing reality. To change something, build a new model that makes the existing model obsolete."
Buckminster Fuller

At some point, many of us stop trying to fit in. Not because we suddenly become brave, but because we become tired. Tired of adjusting, of softening, of wondering whether we're the problem. And when that happens, a question starts to surface: why did we try so hard in the first place?

This part of the book is about that turning point.

It's about the moment you realize that maybe the problem was never you. That perhaps the friction you felt wasn't a personal failure, but a mismatch between who you are and the expectations, the cultures, and the leadership models that were built for someone else.

If Part 1 was about reclaiming who you are, and Part 2 was about reshaping how you lead without abandoning yourself, then Part 3 is about something bigger. It's about questioning the rules altogether. It's about asking whether the standards you've been measuring yourself against were ever fair to begin with. It's about questioning the systems that made so many of us feel behind, not good enough or unsuited for leadership in the first place. It's about leading from who you are, as you are, rather than who you were told to become.

The world has changed, but many workplaces have not. We still celebrate early achievement and question anyone whose growth doesn't follow a straight line. We're still rewarding visibility over depth and we're still expecting people to compartmentalize their grief, their growth, their healing, and show up as if none of it exists.

We call that professionalism, but that version of professionalism was built around a narrow definition of who belongs. It was never designed for people who are different and for complexity. If we want something else, something more sustainable and more honest, then challenging these systems can't be someone else's job, it has to be ours.

And this shift has already begun. We see more people succeed later in life and we see more people following nonlinear career paths. We see leaders speak more openly about grief, mental health, and the realities of being human at work. And these examples are quietly proving something important: you don't need to be loud to be influential, you don't need to follow the template to lead effectively, and you don't need to sacrifice your humanity to be taken seriously.

This part of the book explores what happens when we stop asking how to fit in and start asking how to lead on our own terms.

It unfolds through three rules:

Rule 8: Success Has No Expiry Date - A reminder that there's no universal timeline for achievement, and that growth, reinvention, and leadership aren't limited by age or stage. Success doesn't run out, and you're not late.

Rule 9: You Don't Need Permission - An exploration of how much of what we're waiting for was never required in the first place. This rule is about reclaiming agency, trusting your judgment, and acting without waiting to be chosen, approved, or authorized.

Rule 10: Lead Anyway - A call to step forward without guarantees, certainty, or perfection. Leadership does not begin once everything feels safe or clear, it begins the moment you choose to act anyway.

Together, these rules are about changing the game, not burning it down, but by refusing to keep playing by rules that were never designed with us in mind in the first place.

For a long time, many of us believed we had to adapt ourselves to belong, we had to tone ourselves down, wait for our turn and follow the template. But what this book has been quietly building toward is something else entirely. Leadership doesn't require you to become someone new, it asks you to stop contorting yourself to fit systems that were never built with you in mind.

Part 3 is about what happens when you stop asking for permission, stop apologizing for your timing and stop measuring yourself against standards that don't reflect your depth, your experience or your humanity.

You don't need to fake it to belong and you don't need to wait to be chosen. You don't need to change who you are to lead. And once you finish these rules, you'll be ready to write your own.

Rule 8: Success Has No Expiry Date

"It's never too late to be what you might have been."
George Eliot

In many Western cultures, we're obsessed with early achievement. Forbes 30 Under 30, headlines about the youngest CEO or the youngest self-made billionaire, teenagers building massive YouTube followings, MrBeast becoming one of the most influential creators in the world before turning thirty, young founders making millions through dropshipping, gaming, streaming or content creation before they've even finished school. We've come to treat early success as a signal of greater potential. If someone rises quickly, we assume they're more capable, more driven or simply more destined for leadership.

Over time, we begin to treat early success as proof of greater potential, as if rising quickly signals that someone is more driven, more intelligent or somehow more suited for leadership than those whose careers unfold more slowly, and without really noticing it we start assuming that faster must mean better.

I see it in professionals who are barely thirty and already worried they're falling behind. They scroll LinkedIn and see a peer promoted to manager or handed a bigger scope, and suddenly the question isn't "What kind of work do I want to do?" but *"Am I already too late?"* I've coached people who are doing good work, learning, growing and contributing, and yet they feel uneasy and worried. They're afraid that if they don't advance now, they'll miss their window. That if they don't get promoted this year, they will slowly become invisible and someone will assume they've plateaued. As if staying in the same role for too long becomes evidence against you and it makes others quietly question your potential.

And I recognize this feeling because I felt it too. I spent much of my thirties worried about falling behind. I worked hard, not only because I cared about the work, but because I wanted to stay relevant, I wanted to fit in and I wanted my career to look *"on track."* Every time someone my age got promoted or expanded their scope, I compared timelines. I questioned myself. Was I visible enough, ambitious enough, strategic enough?

And if I am honest, it was not only about ambition, it was about masking. Part of how I blended into corporate environments was by hitting the milestones and making sure my trajectory looked right on paper. I believed that if I slowed down, paused or stayed in one place for too long, people might start looking more closely, and if they looked more closely, they might see the ways in which I did not quite fit the mold.

The more I have reflected on this need to stay "on track," the more I've realized that it was not just personal insecurity, it was something I had learned. We are taught early on to move fast, to prove ourselves quickly and to show progress before anyone starts doubting us, and we internalize the idea that potential peaks young and that anything that doesn't accelerate within a certain timeframe must mean something about our ability.

But what if the timeline you're chasing was never yours to begin with?

Amancio Ortega, born in a working-class family in northwest Spain, left school at 14 to work as a delivery boy for a shirtmaker. For decades, he quietly studied the fashion business from the inside out. He didn't launch Zara, the clothing store chain, until age 39, and he didn't create Inditex, the world's largest fashion retailer, until nearly a decade later. His success was not a rapid rise, it was gradual and built on experience.[74]

Toni Morrison was 39 when her debut novel *The Bluest Eye* was published, and she wrote in the early mornings while raising two sons and working full time. Her work was rejected by several publishers before gaining traction. She was 56 when she won the Pulitzer, and 62 when she won the Nobel Prize in Literature. Her career does not fit the story that brilliance must be discovered young to be valid.[75]

Harland Sanders, better known as Colonel Sanders, failed at multiple careers, from farming to ferry boating, before he started cooking fried chicken in a roadside service station in Kentucky. At age 65, with a $105 social security check and a recipe, he began franchising what would become Kentucky Fried Chicken. He didn't become a global icon until his late sixties. He used to say, *"I made a resolve then that I was going to amount to something if I could. And no hours, nor amount of labor, nor money would deter me."*[76]

Vera Wang, who had been a competitive figure skater and then a fashion editor at Vogue for 15 years, didn't enter the bridal design world until she was 40. She opened her first boutique after being frustrated with the lack of options for her own wedding dress. Today, her brand is synonymous with luxury bridalwear and she often jokes that being *"late to the party"* helped her understand what real women wanted.[77]

We talk constantly about prodigies and disruptors, and we forget how many people build something meaningful later, after they have lived through caregiving, divorce, illness, reinvention, doubt and failure. We forget that experience is not a delay, it's part of the preparation. Not everyone accelerates early, and not everyone can, because life is rarely linear. Some of us are raising children, rebuilding after loss, managing our health, supporting parents or simply taking longer to understand who we are before we are ready to lead with clarity.

I was in my late thirties when I started writing publicly and sharing my ideas. I was forty when I became a VP. I was forty two when I stopped trying to perform someone else's version of leadership and began the slower and more uncomfortable process of leading as myself while unmasking. None of that happened early and none of it followed a spectacular trajectory. And yet when it happened, I was more ready for it than I would have been ten years earlier.

There's no universal timeline for leadership and there's no professional expiration date attached to your potential. The pace at which your career unfolds doesn't invalidate your ability to lead, and the years that looked slow or uncertain often become the years that built the depth, steadiness and judgment you will later rely on.

The Myth of the Timeline

Somewhere along the way, we started measuring success by speed. We began idolizing prodigies, obsessing over 30-under-30 lists and celebrating the youngest CEOs, the fastest growing companies, and the early achievers who seem to have it all figured out without before life has even had time to shape them. Over time, this created a quiet but powerful story that tells us that if success hasn't happened yet, it might never happen at all. That there's a window for ambition, a deadline for leadership, an expiry date for success and that once it closes, you're simply too late.

But that story isn't only inaccurate, it's harmful to everyone. Success doesn't come with a deadline and certainly doesn't expire. Yet, the pressure to arrive by a certain age quietly shapes how many of us see ourselves. It fuels impostor syndrome, creates a constant sense of being behind and it discourages anyone whose path has been nonlinear, interrupted or unconventional. For introverts, caregivers, career shifters, late diagnosed neurodivergents, immigrants, and women navigating workplace bias, timelines often look very different. Not because of a lack of talent or ambition, but because life itself demanded something else first.

We treat *"on time"* as if it were a universal standard, but it isn't. The timeline most of us measure ourselves against was built around uninterrupted careers, stable health, traditional family structures and access to opportunity. It assumes that everyone can move forward at the same pace, without pauses, without detours and without systemic barriers. That standard was never neutral, and it was never designed for nonlinear lives.

For many of us, it takes longer not because we're slower, but because we're doing more than just learning our craft, we're surviving and we're unlearning who we were told to be. We're masking in rooms that were never designed for us and we're burning out in environments that reward overwork but punish authenticity. We're carrying invisible labor, decoding social cues, suppressing sensory overload, and navigating systems where our natural rhythms are mistaken for weakness rather than recognized as difference.

If you're late diagnosed, you may have spent decades trying to thrive while misreading your own needs. If you're neurodivergent or introverted, you may have spent years hiding your wiring just to appear professional. If you belong to a marginalized group, you may have had to work twice as hard for half the recognition. The result of all this is not delay, it's resilience.

You didn't take longer because you lacked ability, you took longer because you were navigating systems that weren't built with you in mind in the first place. And the fact that you're still here, still curious and still wanting to build something meaningful says something about your capacity, not your timeline.

And research supports this reality. A study published in *Nature* examined artistic, cultural and scientific careers and found that so called *"hot streaks,"* periods of highest impact and creativity, are not concentrated at the beginning of a career but can occur at any stage.[78] In other words, major accomplishments are not reserved for young people. High impact moments appear unpredictably rather than on a fixed schedule, which challenges the assumption that brilliance peaks early. Similarly, research published in *American Economic Review: Insights* found that while popular culture often glorifies the young tech founder, the average age of founders behind high growth startups is 45, and the likelihood of building a successful high growth company actually increases into midlife.[79]

We don't hear these stories often, we don't glorify the slow burn and we don't celebrate reinvention. We don't talk about the artist that picked up a brush at 50, the author who publishes her first novel at the age of 60 or the engineer who changed career at 40. And yet, these stories are everywhere and are quietly unfolding beyond the noise of the 22-year-old successful CEO headline.

Barbara Strauch, in *The Secret Life of the Grown Up Brain*, highlights that while certain abilities like processing speed may slow with age, other capacities, including emotional regulation, strategic thinking and complex problem solving, often strengthen over time, precisely the qualities most needed in leadership, creativity and innovation.[80]

Neurodivergent people, in particular, often operate on nonlinear developmental timelines. We don't all peak in our twenties. Some of us don't find our voice until 35, some of us don't unmask until 45 and some of us only begin to thrive when we finally give ourselves permission to stop performing and start building something aligned with who we actually are.

That isn't being late, it's arriving when your experience and your timing finally align.

Success Takes Time When You're Busy Surviving

There's a particular sense of panic that sets in when you feel like you're falling behind as if there was a master clock ticking somewhere and you missed the memo. You scroll through social media and see 28 years old scaling their startups successfully, founders raising millions, authors publishing their third book by the age of 30, an acquaintance of yours getting promoted once again and an old classmate celebrating yet another career milestone on LinkedIn. And as you scroll, a quiet question creeps in *"Did I miss my window?"*.

I've opened LinkedIn and felt a rush of comparison tighten my chest, wondering how far behind I'd fallen. I've compared my accomplishments to those of acquaintances and strangers, felt mediocre about my own professional life, and said unkind things to myself. I've sat in room full of confident voices, watching people move through corporate spaces with an ease I could never replicate. For the longest time, I assumed, like many of us, that the problem was me. That I was too slow, too uncertain, too different and that my detours and hesitations somehow disqualified me from success. What I didn't understand then is that many of us aren't slow, we're just surviving and trying to find our ways.

When you're neurodivergent, introverted, living with chronic anxiety, grief or long-term stress, the work doesn't move at your speed. You need to constantly adjust, accommodate and mask. You learn to work twice as hard just to appear like you're keeping up. You become highly skilled at performance and deeply exhausted by the cost of constantly adjusting, accommodating and masking. While others seem to sprint towards milestones, you're still figuring out where and how to stand without burning out.

A few years ago, I remember standing in my kitchen trying to explain to my now ex-wife why I felt so behind in my career. On paper, I was doing pretty well. I had years of professional experience, I had a leadership role, I had reached milestones that looked impressive from the outside, and yet, I felt hollow. I was realizing that I had spent years trying to meet what I believed was everyone else's expectations of what professional success and leadership should look like. That it should be polished, certain, tireless and filled with continuous success. I had learned how to fit in, but I hadn't learned how to lead as myself.

For those of us who are high masking or neurodivergent or both, it often takes longer to find an authentic path. Not because we lack ambition, but because unmasking and discovering who we truly are, once we allow ourselves, is rarely immediate. Many of us have worn a mask for so long that we no longer know who we are without it. Taking it off isn't a single decision, it's a gradual and long process. We have to relearn what actually energizes us, what feels sustainable, what our real ambitions are, what we want from life, and what kind of leadership we want to practice. And to learn all of this, we first have to unlearn decades of adaptation.

Research from the World Health Organization and Gallup confirms that workplace stress and burnout are widespread and disproportionately impact women globally.[55,58] When you layer on masking, systemic exclusion and the constant pressure to adapt in non-inclusive environments, the cost becomes even heavier for neurodivergent professionals. That kind of stress slows people down, not because they lack drive or ambition, but because they're operating in systems that were never designed for their brains or bodies.

Dr Devon Price captures this idea powerfully in *Unmasking Autism*, arguing that there is no universal timeline for life and that growth happens in the order and at the pace that works for each person. [81]

That idea changed something for me, because I realized that when you've spent years adapting just to get through the day, moving fast isn't a goal anymore. What matters is to understand yourself, to figure out what you can sustain, how to build a life and a career that doesn't require constant self-suppression. And I realized that leadership that grows from a place of self-understanding and self-respect may look slower from the outside, but it's steadier, more grounded and far less fragile.

And once I saw that, I also started noticing how many stories we rarely tell because they don't promote the myth of youthful success.

Consider Anna Mary Robertson Moses, better known as Grandma Moses. She didn't begin painting until she was in her late seventies, after arthritis made embroidery too painful. By the time she passed away at 101, her work had been exhibited internationally and featured on the cover of *TIME* Magazine.[82] Or take Te Ping Chen, a journalist who spent years reporting for *The Wall Street Journal*, whose debut short story collection *Land of Big Numbers* was published after a long career in journalism and years of writing alongside her reporting.[83]

These aren't stories of people who were late, they're stories of people who began when their circumstances allowed them to.

For many women, especially those balancing caregiving, career, systemic barriers, and misogynistic expectations, success doesn't always look like a straight line. For neurodivergent professionals, burnout delays progress because we're busy managing sensory overwhelm, decoding unspoken rules, compensating in environments that were never designed for our nervous systems, and learning how to ask for what we need. None of these challenges and accomplishments show up on a CV and none of this fit neatly into a timeline, but all of it shapes who we become.

Looking back, I can see that much of what I once interpreted as being behind was actually preparation. I was learning boundaries before I had language for them, I was learning discernment before I trusted my instincts and I was learning what kind of leader I didn't want to be. It took time and it had to. I didn't need to move faster, I needed to arrive more honestly.

And this is something I wish I had known earlier in my career and in my life. I wish I had realized earlier on that blooming late doesn't mean blooming wrong, that speed has no moral value and that your pace isn't a failure of ambition, but often a reflection of how much you've been carrying.

If you're reading this feeling like everyone else has already arrived, let me say this clearly: you're not behind, you're in process. And process takes time.

Tips and Tools: Redefining "On Time"

1. Reclaim Your Metrics

Most of us are chasing success using someone else's measure of success: titles, promotions, salaries, visibility, follower counts. These external markers are loud, visible and easy to measure, which makes them socially powerful. They allow comparison, they signal progress and they create the illusion of certainty.

But they rarely capture what actually feels meaningful or sustainable for the individuals.

When speed becomes the main way we measure progress, we stop paying attention to depth. When visibility becomes the way we judge leadership, we overlook steadiness and judgment. And when promotion becomes the proof of competence, we start tying our worth to how quickly we move rather than how well we lead.

For introverts, success may look like depth rather than exposure. For neurodivergent leaders, it may look like working in flow without constant masking. For someone rebuilding after burnout or navigating a complex season of life, success may look like stability, clarity and energy rather than expansion.

If your metrics ignore your nervous system, your values and your actual capacity, you will always feel behind someone.

Reclaiming your metrics means deciding what success feels like from the inside, not just how it looks from the outside. It means defining progress in a way that reflects the life you are actually living, not the one that is most rewarded publicly.

Start by asking yourself:

- What have I been using as proof that I am "on track"?
- Which of those metrics are mine and which are borrowed?
- What kind of progress would feel steady rather than urgent?
- If no one else could see my career, how would I define success?

When you change the metric, the urgency changes with it, because you are no longer competing on a clock that wasn't designed for you.

2. Track Invisible Labor

Not all work shows up on a calendar or a task list. Masking, decoding social dynamics, managing executive function, navigating overstimulating environments, or constantly adjusting to unspoken expectations all require real effort. When this invisible labor goes unacknowledged, it's easy to underestimate your workload and blame yourself for being tired without knowing why. On paper, your week might look manageable, but in reality, you may have spent a significant portion of your energy on adapting rather than executing.

Timelines assume equal starting conditions and equal cognitive bandwidth. They assume that if two people have the same title and the same hours, they are expending the same effort. That simply isn't true.

Tracking invisible labor isn't about productivity optimization, it's about self-understanding. By doing so, it gives you a language to understand your efforts and what's usually dismissed or ignored. By doing so, you can make sense of why certain days feel heavier than others, even when the workload looks the same or "reasonable" on paper. When you name the hidden cost of the work, you stop interpreting fatigue as weakness and delay as incompetence.

Instead of only tracking what you produce, begin noticing what each part of your day requires from you internally. Pay attention to which interactions demand extra self monitoring, which environments increase sensory strain, which conversations require you to soften or sharpen parts of yourself to fit in, and which tasks feel straightforward without constant adjustment. When you review your day, don't just evaluate output, reflect on the amount of regulation, adaptation and emotional effort that came with it.

You might ask yourself:

- What part of my work requires me to adapt more than it requires my skills?
- Where am I spending energy that no one else can see?
- Am I judging my output without considering what it costs me?

As you become more honest about that hidden effort, your interpretation of your own pace begins to shift. What once looked like slowness may reveal itself as sustained compensation. What once felt like falling behind may turn out to be the result of carrying more than what's visible. When you account for the real cost of your work, the story you tell yourself about your capacity often becomes more accurate and far less self critical.

3. Redefine Milestones

Most career milestones are inherited by the systems we live in and societal expectations, they're not chosen by us individuals. We graduate by a certain age, get promoted every few years, reach peak early, etc. These timelines are treated as neutral, but they quietly assume uninterrupted progress, stable health, and lives free from major disruption. Let's be honest, real lives rarely look like that.

When your path includes burnout, grief, caregiving, immigration, career shifts, late diagnosis or long periods of self-doubt, your timeline will look different. Not because you lack ambition, but because your capacity has been directed toward survival, adaptation and rebuilding.

Redefining milestones means expanding what counts as growth. Healing from chronic stress, learning how to set boundaries, leaving environments that required constant self-suppression, figuring out what you can actually sustain and rebuilding confidence after years of masking. These shifts may not change your title immediately, but they change your leadership.

If you only recognize vertical movement as progress, you will miss the depth you are building horizontally. And depth, over time, often becomes the difference between someone who rises quickly and someone who lasts.

You might ask yourself:

- Which milestones do I believe I should have reached by now?
- Who defined those milestones for me?
- What did this slower phase force me to learn?
- What capacity have I built that doesn't show up on my CV?

Instead of asking whether you have advanced fast enough, ask what this phase of your life required you to learn. Instead of asking whether you are late, ask what capacity you now have that you didn't have five years ago.

When you redefine milestones, the timeline loses its authority, because you stop treating acceleration as the only evidence of growth.

4. Expand Your Reference Point

Comparison narrows perspective, especially when the only people you compare yourself to are those who rose early, fast or visibly. If the stories you consume are all about acceleration, your brain starts treating speed as normal and delay as failure. Over time, that creates urgency where there doesn't need to be any.

One way to interrupt that pattern is to deliberately expand the reference points you use for success. Instead of only noticing early prodigies or fast promotions, begin paying attention to people whose paths unfolded slowly, changed direction, paused, or deepened over time. These don't need to be famous figures, they can be colleagues, mentors, friends or leaders you've observed from a distance. What matters isn't their visibility, but the reminder that growth rarely follows a single straight line.

This isn't about collecting inspiration, it's about recalibrating your nervous system and expectations. When your brain regularly sees examples of nonlinear progress, reinvention and later emergence, it becomes easier to believe that your own pace is legitimate.

You might ask yourself:

- Who do I know whose career didn't follow a straight line?
- What did time give them that speed couldn't?
- What shifts in me when I remember that multiple timelines are possible?

When you widen your reference points, urgency softens. The pressure to "catch up" loses some of its authority and your timeline begins to feel less like a race and more like a process.

5. Design for Energy, Not Ego

It's easy to build a career around what looks impressive rather than what's sustainable. The role that sounds important, the visibility that signals relevance and the pace that proves you are progressing. Over time, you can end up structuring your work around external validation instead of internal capacity.

Timeline pressure feeds this pattern. When you're worried about falling behind, saying yes can feel safer than slowing down. You accept opportunities because they signal progress, not because they fit your life or your nervous system. You stretch yourself to maintain an image of momentum, even when your energy is quietly eroding.

Designing your time and career for energy means taking your capacity seriously. It means asking not only whether you can do something, but whether you can do it repeatedly without burning out. Leadership isn't just about what you can deliver once, it's about whether your way of working allows you to stay steady, thoughtful and present over time.

Energy isn't a bonus, it's what makes consistency possible.

You might ask yourself:

- What parts of my work leave me feeling grounded rather than depleted?
- Where am I maintaining momentum at the expense of recovery?
- If I keep working this way for the next few years, what will it cost me?

Designing for energy doesn't make you less ambitious, it makes your ambition sustainable. And when your ambition is sustainable, your timeline becomes something you can actually manage yourself rather than something you're constantly trying to catch-up to.

Visual Summary

Practice	What It Looks Like	Why It Works
1. Reclaim Your Metrics	Defining success by what feels meaningful and sustainable to you rather than by speed, titles or visibility. Replacing borrowed milestones with internal measures of progress.	Reduces comparison and urgency. Weakens the pressure of external timelines. Restores agency and self-trust.
2. Track Invisible Labor	Acknowledging the cognitive and emotional effort required to adapt, mask and regulate in addition to executing tasks. Evaluating not only output but cost.	Prevents misinterpreting fatigue as incompetence. Makes your pace more understandable. Reduces self-criticism.

3. Redefine Milestones	Expanding what counts as growth to include healing, boundary setting, discernment and sustainability, not only promotions or acceleration.	Challenges the assumption that progress must be linear. Validates nonlinear paths. Reframes slower phases as development.
4. Expand Your Reference Points	Deliberately noticing careers that unfolded slowly or nonlinearly instead of only early or fast success stories.	Reduces scarcity thinking. Normalizes multiple timelines. Calms urgency triggered by comparison.
5. Design for Energy, Not Ego	Structuring work around sustainable capacity rather than image or momentum. Choosing consistency over short-term impression.	Protects long-term performance. Prevents burnout driven by timeline anxiety. Supports steadier leadership over time.

Micro-Practice: Loosen the Timeline

Timeline anxiety usually shows up as urgency. A sense that you should already be further, that something needs to move faster and that if you don't accelerate now, you'll fall behind.

This practice isn't about calming yourself down, it's about questioning the clock you're trying to follow.

Set aside five quiet minutes. No phone, no scrolling and no distraction.

Write down the answer to these two questions:

- What do I feel pressure to achieve right now?
- Who would I disappoint if I slowed down?
- If I stopped trying to catch up, what would I focus on instead?
- If this didn't need to prove anything, how would it change the way I work and the way I feel?

Notice what shifts when speed is no longer the main reference point.

Finish by completing this sentence:
"At this stage of my life, success looks like…"

Keep that sentence visible for the next week and let it guide at least one decision.

Practical Quick Phrases

Use these internally or out loud when comparison or urgency starts shaping your decisions.

To interrupt comparison:

- *"I'm not behind, I'm on a different path."*
- *"Their timing has nothing to say about mine."*
- *"I don't need to match someone else's pace to be legitimate."*

When urgency starts to take over:

- *"I don't need to rush to be taken seriously."*
- *"Speed isn't proof of competence."*
- *"I'm allowed to let this take the time it actually needs."*

When you feel "late"':

- *"I'm arriving with experience."*
- *"My timing reflects my life, not my worth."*
- *"Nothing about my leadership has an expiry date."*

To bring the focus back to choice:

- *"I get to define what success looks like now."*
- *"I can choose depth over speed."*
- *"I don't need permission to move at my pace."*

These aren't affirmations meant to deny reality. They're interruptions, they help you question the clock you're obeying and bring you back to deliberate choices instead of staying stuck in the reflex of urgency.

Checklist: What Will You Try This Week?

Choose one or two and test them in real time:

- The next time you open LinkedIn or compare yourself to someone, pause and say out loud what you're reacting to: comparison, urgency, or pressure to catch up. Don't scroll further until you've named it.
- Pick one success metric you've been quietly using to judge yourself this month. Write it down. Then replace it with a metric you actually believe in and use that instead for the rest of the week.
- At the end of one workday, write down not only what you did, but what it cost you in regulation, adaptation or masking. Let that information shape how you plan the next day.
- Before saying yes to one request this week, ask yourself whether you're choosing it because it fits your capacity or because it signals progress.
- Once this week, deliberately allow something to take longer than planned without rushing to compensate. Notice what happens when you don't try to prove momentum.

This checklist isn't about catching up, it's about slowing the story down enough to choose differently.

Closing: It's Never Too Late to Become the Leader You Needed

For the longest time, I believed there was a clock in the background of my life. An invisible countdown I was constantly measuring myself against. If I had not *"made it"* by a certain age, published something meaningful, reached a certain title or figured out who I was supposed to be, then I'd somehow failed. Failed at what? Failed at life. I told myself that if clarity, confidence or success hadn't arrived by 35 or 40, then I must have missed my chance.

But I was wrong, and I can see that clearly now.

Success isn't linear, it's not a race and it doesn't come with a deadline. What looks like delay is often development and what looks like a detour is often preparation.

I became a VP in my forties, but if it had happened in my fifties, it would have been just as fine. I only began speaking publicly about being neurodivergent after decades of masking. I'm writing a book later than I once imagined I would. And all of this is better. It's better this way because I'm better for it. Not because I suddenly have everything figured out, but because I stopped measuring my worth by speed and started valuing depth instead. I'm still becoming, and that's not a flaw. It's what a life actually looks like when you stop performing it and just live it.

Consider Esther Perel, a renowned and popular psychologist. She did not become a global voice on relationships, intimacy and power dynamics in her twenties. Her authority was built over decades of clinical practice, immigration, listening deeply to thousands of stories and refining her thinking long before the world amplified her voice. Profiles of her career show how her influence grew slowly from accumulated experience rather than early disruption.[84] Her work carries weight because it's grounded in time, not urgency. It resonates because it was shaped by complexity, not speed.

That pattern repeats more often than we admit. Research shows that creative and professional *"hot streaks"* can emerge at multiple points in a career rather than clustering at the beginning.[78] Studies on entrepreneurship consistently demonstrate that successful founders are, on average, well into midlife rather than fresh out of university.[79] Experience compounds, perspective matures and judgment deepens. None of that fits neatly into a culture that celebrates youth as shorthand for potential.

This is what we miss when we obsess over early success. It's easy to panic when your timeline doesn't match the world's expectations, especially if you're wired differently, if you've burned out, started over, taken breaks for healing, caregiving or survival, or spent years adapting in systems that don't fit with who you are. It's easy to feel exposed when your path includes chapters you can't summarize in a tidy LinkedIn update. But those chapters aren't gaps, they're context, they sharpen boundaries, they deepen empathy and they shape leaders who are grounded and empathetic rather than performative.

You're not late because you took time to understand yourself. You're not behind because your life includes disruption. And you're not less capable because your growth wasn't visible early.

The work you're doing now, whether it is external and measurable or internal and quiet, isn't time wasted, it's foundation and it's you becoming someone who can lead with more clarity and more steadiness than you could have ten years ago.

Let the world rush if it wants to and let others peak early. There's no expiry date attached to your potential, and there's no deadline on becoming the leader you needed when you were younger.

Rule 9: You Don't Need Permission

"Power is not given to you. You have to take it."
Beyoncé

I spent years waiting to be told I was ready. Waiting for someone more senior, more certain or more established to look at me and confirm that I was allowed to step forward, that I had earned my stripes and I had proven myself. I thought there would be a moment when the doubts would quiet down because someone else had finally validated me. And I waited for that external confirmation to arrive, as if leadership required a formal invitation.

At some point, I realized something uncomfortable but freeing: no one was coming to declare me ready. No title would erase insecurity, no certification would eliminate doubt and no senior leader was going to hand me a final stamp of legitimacy. The sense of arrival I was waiting for was never going to happen. And that's because there isn't a final gatekeeper or a formal moment where someone confirms you've earned the right. There's only you, your values, your judgment and your willingness to act before you feel fully prepared.

When I became a VP, I still felt like an impostor. The role had been granted to me, my title was real and I had been given the authority. But the permission I was waiting for didn't arrive. I kept expecting a shift that would make me suddenly feel entitled to lead, but that shift didn't happen. I continued to overprepare for every meeting and constantly questioned my instincts. I told myself that if I could just become more confident, more polished, more like other leaders I saw around me, then I'd finally feel like I belonged.

The longer I waited for permission, the more I deferred to other people's judgment instead of my own. Over time, it became clear that no one was going to hand me legitimacy. There was no crown and no ceremony that would finally make me feel authorized. I had to stop waiting for reassurance that I was doing leadership "the right way" and accept that there would be no final confirmation. I was already in the role, I was already leading and the work I had to do was to learn to trust myself while doing it.

And this is where the distinction matters.

In most workplaces, formal leadership roles are given, titles are assigned and someone decides who gets promoted and who doesn't. But leadership itself doesn't begin at the promotion. It begins the moment you take responsibility, speak with conviction, make decisions aligned with your values or influence the direction of a room or a project. You can hold the title and still wait for permission internally and you can have no title at all and still be leading in practice.

And as I began to see that, I understood something else. This waiting for permission wasn't a personal flaw, it was conditioning.

Most of us are taught, explicitly or subtly, that leadership is something you're chosen for. That authority must be earned through patience, compliance, perfection and timing. That you must wait until you're endorsed or approved before you step forward. This message lands especially hard on women, neurodivergent professionals, minorities and anyone who doesn't resemble the default image of leadership they see around them. It lands hard because we learn to delay ourselves and to shrink our ambition until it feels acceptable to ask *"Am I allowed?"* instead of *"Why not me?"*

This rule, *You Don't Need Permission*, begins here. It begins with the moment you realize that the permission you're waiting for isn't external, it's internal. That even when the title arrives, the legitimacy you're looking for doesn't automatically follow and that waiting for it has been quietly costing you your voice, your agency, and your influence.

Viola Davis knows this moment well. Davis is one of the most respected actors of her generation. A Juilliard trained performer, she is an Emmy, Grammy, Oscar and Tony Award winner. Yet for decades, her career was marked by rejection, typecasting and being told she didn't fit the industry's narrow definition of marketable. Her breakthrough film role came in her forties, in *Doubt*. Even then, she has spoken openly about how often she was encouraged to make herself smaller, quieter and more palatable.

In her memoir *Finding Me*, Davis writes candidly about years of rejection, internalized invisibility and the pressure to fit an industry that had limited space for Black women who didn't fit conventional beauty standards. She describes the emotional cost of trying to earn recognition in spaces that questioned her worth altogether. The turning point wasn't a single award or breakthrough role, it was the decision to stop measuring her value by whether the system approved of her. Instead of continuing to shape herself around what casting directors or studios considered acceptable, she began making choices rooted in her own standards. She became more deliberate about the roles she pursued, more honest about what she would no longer tolerate and more grounded in how she wanted to be seen. Instead of waiting to be fully seen, she began grounding her authority in her own voice and experience. Her legitimacy didn't begin with permission, it strengthened when she stopped seeking it.[85]

Greta Thunberg offers another powerful example of what it looks like to lead without permission. At fifteen, Thunberg began striking alone in front of the Swedish Parliament. She had no institutional backing, no political power, no adult permission. She was told she was too young, too emotional, too radical, and too inconvenient. She acted anyway.

What began as a solitary protest became a global climate movement. Thunberg addressed the United Nations, confronted world leaders, and reshaped the language of climate accountability. She didn't wait for the credentials nor did she wait to be invited into power. She treated moral clarity as sufficient authority, and acted accordingly. Her leadership didn't come from age, status or approval, it came from conviction and action.[86]

What both stories reveal is something uncomfortable but essential: permission is often granted after the fact and legitimacy tends to follow courage, not precede it.

And yet, many of us keep waiting. We wait to be picked, to be perfect and to be certain. But leadership isn't a title you receive once you're deemed worthy, it's a decision you make when you stop outsourcing your authority.

You don't need permission to lead, all you need is to trust yourself enough to begin.

Authority Is Claimed, Not Given

In most workplaces, authority looks official. It comes with a title change, a new line on the org chart and a public announcement. But the ability to influence, to set direction and to shape decisions rarely begins on the day that announcement goes out.

We tell ourselves that leadership begins when someone higher up decides we're ready. That there's a sequence to it. First we prove ourselves, then we get approved and then we're allowed to lead. That logic makes sense on paper because promotions do work that way. Someone chooses, someone signs off and someone announces it.

But that's not how authority feels from the inside.

From the inside, it usually starts much smaller. It starts when you say the thing no one else is saying in a meeting. When you make a decision and stand by it even though you're not entirely comfortable. When you stop deferring to the loudest voice in the room and trust your own read of the situation. Those moments rarely come with applause and they don't come with a title change, but they are leadership in practice.

This is where many capable people misread themselves. They think the hesitation they feel means they shouldn't act yet and they assume they need to feel completely certain before they speak or fully confident before they decide. They believe permission comes before action, when in reality action is what creates legitimacy. So they wait and they keep waiting for that internal click that tells them they're ready.

But as many of us are aware, that click rarely comes.

Leadership identity isn't something you build privately and then unveil once it's perfect. It forms while you're doing the work and it develops while you're making imperfect decisions, speaking while slightly unsure and taking responsibility before you feel perfect.

Herminia Ibarra's research shows exactly this. People don't become leaders because they finally feel ready, they become leaders by stepping into new behaviors and allowing their identity to evolve in response. In *Act Like a Leader, Think Like a Leader*, she argues that we grow into leadership through action, not through waiting for internal certainty or external endorsement. Confidence develops as we take responsibility, experiment and engage at a higher level. It follows behavior far more often than it precedes it.[87]

And yet, many of us have been trained to do the opposite.

As women, as introverts, as neurodivergent professionals, and as people navigating environments that were never designed with us in mind, we're often socialized into restraint rather than initiative. We learn that authority must be earned slowly, carefully, and visibly, through patience, compliance, and perfection. We're encouraged to wait until our certainty is unquestionable and our competence undeniable, even though that standard is rarely applied evenly. Some people are allowed to experiment publicly, to be wrong, to grow out loud and still be seen as leadership material. Others are scrutinized more closely, judged more harshly or expected to prove themselves repeatedly before being granted the same legitimacy. Over time, this teaches capable people to hesitate, not because they lack insight or readiness, but because they have learned that stepping forward carries risk if you don't fit the expected mold.

This conditioning isn't neutral and it has concrete effects. It determines who feels entitled to speak, who second-guesses themselves, and who stays silent despite having insight the room desperately needs. It pushes people with lived experience, pattern recognition, and systems awareness to hold back, to wait for certainty that never arrives, and to underestimate the value of what they already know.

History gives us plenty of examples of what happens when someone stops waiting.

Alexandria Ocasio-Cortez is a clear example of what it looks like to stop waiting for permission. Before entering politics, she was working as a bartender in New York. She had no traditional political pedigree, no powerful network backing her, and no signal that she was "next in line." At 28, she challenged a ten term incumbent in a primary race most people assumed she would lose quietly.[88]

She didn't wait until she felt fully qualified or until the system made space for her. She stepped forward grounded in her lived experience and her critique of inequality, despite lacking the traditional credentials that usually signal political readiness. And in doing so, she disrupted the idea that authority only belongs to those who have already been sanctioned by power.

What made her leadership visible wasn't permission, seniority, or polish, it was the decision to act as if her voice already mattered. People didn't decide she was legitimate first and then followed her, they followed her because she moved.

Moments like this show something we don't like to admit: legitimacy often comes after action, not before it. Those who change systems don't wait until they feel credible, they move first, and credibility reorganizes around them.

This doesn't mean ignoring expertise or hierarchy, and it doesn't mean pretending to know what you don't know. Leading without permission isn't about ego, it's about recognizing that your experience, your judgment and your values already qualify you to contribute. Waiting for certainty can feel responsible, but very often it becomes a habit of holding yourself back.

Tara Mohr writes about this in *Playing Big*. She argues that many women and marginalized voices silence themselves long before anyone externally does. They use language carefully, they soften their opinions and they wait for one more credential, one more endorsement, one more signal that they won't be challenged. Not because they lack insight, but because they've been trained to question their own authority.[89]

If you look at this in a workplace context, it becomes pretty clear what's happening. The hesitation so many capable people carry isn't proof that they're not ready, it's often the result of being in environments where approval is treated as the same thing as legitimacy. Over time, that shapes how you show up. You start holding back, you soften what you really want to say and you delay decisions even when you already know what you think, because you've learned that stepping forward without endorsement can come at a cost.

This is especially true for those who've survived by being agreeable, adaptable or invisible. When you've spent years reading the room and managing reactions, waiting can feel strategic. But there's a point where caution stops being wisdom and starts turning into shrinking yourself.

Leadership doesn't begin when doubt disappears. It begins when you decide that doubt doesn't get to run the show. You can feel unsure and still speak. You can feel exposed and still decide. You can feel nervous and still lead. You don't need to be chosen to contribute, you don't need consensus before you offer your thinking and you don't need someone else's confidence in you before you trust your own judgment.

Rule 9 isn't about forcing yourself forward or pretending you're certain when you're not. It's about noticing how often you've been waiting for a signal that was never required in the first place. It's about recognizing that the authority you've been looking for externally has been available to you internally all along.

You Don't Need Permission to Take Up Space

One of the hardest things to accept is that permission rarely arrives with certainty. There's no internal click, no sudden confidence, no moment where fear quietly disappears and clarity takes over. When you stop waiting, what you often feel first isn't empowerment but exposure. It feels like standing without a safety net and realizing that if things go wrong, there's no one else to point to.

For a long time, that realization terrified me.

Because waiting for permission isn't only about validation, it's also about protection. As long as someone else has authorized you, responsibility feels shared. If you fail, the blame isn't entirely yours. If you succeed, it confirms they were right to choose you.

Letting go of permission means accepting that no one else is going to carry the responsibility for you. It means standing fully in your own judgment, owning your choices without guarantees and accepting that there's no higher authority to defer to if things get uncomfortable.

And that, more than the fear of failure, is what makes waiting so tempting.

When you've spent years adapting, masking, and calibrating yourself to other people's expectations, self-trust doesn't feel natural. It feels reckless, it feels premature and it feels like you're skipping a step you were supposed to complete first.

That's what makes this shift so uncomfortable. You're not just speaking up, you're breaking a pattern that once kept you safe. You're stepping out of a version of yourself that was built around anticipation and caution. And even when you know you're capable, acting without reassurance can feel like exposure.

Even after I understood all of this intellectually, I noticed how often I still hesitated. I'd catch myself asking, *"Is this too much?" "Am I overstepping?" "Is this the right time?"* The pattern didn't disappear just because I could name it. Giving yourself permission, I've now learned, isn't a single decision, it's a daily practice. And sometimes, it's actually an hourly one.

For me, what changed wasn't that I suddenly became fearless or confident. What changed was that I stopped treating doubt as a stop sign and instead I began to see it as information. Although it requires immense courage, I started to let myself speak while uncertain, decide without being completely sure and be visible while still figuring things out.

At first, nothing dramatic happened. No one clapped and no one confirmed I was doing it right. And that, paradoxically, was actually the point. Leadership that depends on permission is fragile because it collapses the moment approval is withdrawn. Leadership rooted in self-trust has a different quality. It's quieter, less performative and far more stable because it doesn't require constant reassurance to exist.

Writer and activist Audre Lorde wrote about this tension decades ago. As a Black lesbian feminist navigating racism, sexism and homophobia, she understood what it meant to measure the cost of speaking in rooms that were not built for her. In Sister Outsider, a collection of her essays and speeches, she reflects on fear not as something that disappears before we act, but as something that often accompanies truth. She argued that waiting until we felt safe or certain would keep us silent indefinitely. The real risk wasn't speaking, it was staying silent and realizing too late what that silence had cost.[90]

While writing this book, I discussed this topic with friends and colleagues and I noticed something else too. When we stop waiting, we don't just change how we show up, but we also change the space around us. Others start to speak up more freely, decisions are made faster and conversations become more honest. Not because we're louder or more charismatic, but because we stop acting as if our voice needs approval to count and this has a ripple effect on the people around us.

Research on psychological safety supports this. Studies from Google's Project Aristotle and later research on psychological safety showed something simple but powerful: teams do better when people feel safe to speak up. Not just the most senior person, not just the loudest voice, but everyone. When authority isn't treated like something that only lives at the top, people contribute more. When one person stops waiting to be approved before speaking, it gives others permission to do the same. Conversations become more direct, decisions improve and people engage more fully.[91]

This is what we rarely talk about when we talk about permission. It isn't about being bold for the sake of it. It's about being grounded and it's about letting your presence be enough, even when it's imperfect, inconvenient or still evolving.

If you're reading this and feeling the familiar tension between wanting to step forward and wanting to stay safe, let me say this clearly:

You don't need to resolve all your doubts before you speak.
You don't need to feel confident before you decide.
You don't need to be certain before you lead.

Permission doesn't arrive when fear disappears. It arrives when you decide fear doesn't get to make the decision for you. And when you make that shift, something changes. You stop asking if you're allowed and you start focusing on what actually needs to be said, done or challenged.

Tips and Tools: Leading Without Permission

1. Build Inner Permission First

You can receive the title, the praise, the promotion and still feel like you're borrowing authority instead of actually owning it. You can be formally in charge and still hesitate before you speak, still look around the room to see who goes first, still wonder whether you've truly earned the right to decide.

The role can change overnight, but the internal doubts don't.

That's because what you're really waiting for isn't another credential, it's the moment you decide that your judgment counts, even when it isn't immediately validated. Inner permission isn't confidence and it's not the absence of doubt. It's the decision to stop asking whether you're allowed and to start acting as if your contribution already matters.

For many of us, waiting has become automatic. We scan the room before we trust ourselves, we soften our opinions before anyone has challenged them and we prepare one more slide, one more argument, one more layer of proof before we move. Building inner permission means noticing that pattern and interrupting it on purpose.

To work with this practically, take a few minutes and reflect on the following:

- Where am I still waiting for someone to confirm something I already know I can handle?
- In which situations do I overprepare because I'm trying to earn the right to speak?
- Where am I editing or shrinking my thinking before it even leaves my mouth?
- If I knew this wouldn't be held against me later, would I move faster or speak sooner?

After you've sat with these questions and written down your answers, turn them into something concrete. Write down the specific permissions you are no longer willing to wait for. Be clear, be specific and name them in plain language.

Keep that note somewhere close, in your notebook, in your bag, folded into your laptop case, wherever you'll actually see it. The point isn't to make a grand statement. The point is to have something to reach for the next time you're in a meeting and feel yourself hesitate, the next time you catch yourself looking around the room for a signal or the next time you start shrinking a point before you've even made it.

When that moment comes, take it out and read what you wrote. Not to convince yourself you're fearless, but to remind yourself that you've already decided you don't need to wait. And this is important because the shift doesn't happen in theory, it happens in that exact moment when you choose not to pause yourself again.

2. Start Small, But Start Now

Once you've stopped waiting for permission in theory, the real work begins in practice. Because even when you've decided you're allowed, your behavior doesn't automatically change. You can believe you're capable and still find yourself hesitating at the exact moment where action is required.

This is where timing matters.

Many capable people don't struggle with insight, they struggle with action. They wait a few extra seconds before speaking, they let one or two people go first or they refine their point internally while the conversation moves on. By the time they're ready, the moment has passed.

That delay becomes a habit. Starting small is about retraining that habit. It's not about becoming louder or more dominant, it's about shortening the gap between thinking and acting.

Instead of asking yourself whether your point is perfectly formed, experiment with speaking when it's eighty percent clear. Instead of waiting until the end of the meeting, try entering the conversation earlier. Instead of polishing your thought into something airtight, allow it to be part of the process.

Reflect on the following:

- How long do I typically wait before I speak in a meeting?
- Do I tend to enter conversations early, or only once others have set the direction?
- Where does my idea usually sit, in my head, on my notes, or actually in the room?
- What would it look like to move my contribution forward by just a few minutes?

Choose one specific situation in the coming days and adjust your timing deliberately. Speak earlier than you normally would or offer the first draft of a thought instead of the final version.

You're not trying to be impressive, you're simply training yourself to act while the moment is still alive.

And this is important because leadership doesn't only depend on what you think, it depends on when you decide to place that thinking into the room.

3. Practice Micro-Visibility

For many people, visibility feels heavy and it can feel like stepping onto a stage. And when visibility feels dramatic and difficult, it's something you start to limit. You save your voice for when it really matters, you wait until your point is strong enough to withstand scrutiny and you treat speaking as an event.

That approach quietly reinforces the idea that your presence needs to be earned each time.

Micro visibility is different. It's about making your presence normal rather than exceptional. It's about showing up in small, consistent ways so that your voice becomes part of the rhythm of the room instead of a rare interruption.

When your voice appears regularly, it stops feeling like a performance and it starts to feel expected. Not because you've become louder, but because you've become consistent.

This isn't about dominating airtime, it's about reducing the emotional charge around being seen and heard. To work with this practically, focus on frequency rather than impact.

Reflect on the following:

- Do I treat speaking as something that needs to be perfectly timed and fully formed?
- How often does my voice appear in meetings compared to how often I'm thinking?
- Am I waiting for my contribution to feel *"important enough"* before I share it?
- What would it look like to make my presence more regular instead of more impressive?

Then choose one small visibility habit and repeat it. Speak within the first part of a meeting, even briefly, offer one observation before the discussion settles, share an early thought instead of the final summary or contribute more than once if you have something relevant to add.

The goal isn't to stand out, it's to stop making visibility such a high stakes moment. Because when your presence becomes familiar, it stops feeling risky. And when it stops feeling risky, you stop treating your voice as something that needs to be carefully rationed.

4. Reframe Self-Doubt as Data

Self-doubt doesn't disappear just because you've decided to stop waiting for permission. In fact, it often gets louder right after you begin acting differently. The moment you speak earlier, decide faster or make your presence more visible, a familiar voice tends to show up: *"Who do you think you are?" "What if you're wrong?" "What if this backfires?"*

Most of us have been trained to treat that voice as a stop sign. But doubt isn't always a warning, sometimes it's simply a sign that you care, that the stakes feel real, or that you're operating at the edge of your comfort zone. Complex decisions create doubt, important conversations create doubt and growth creates doubt.

The presence of doubt doesn't automatically mean you're unqualified, it often means you're engaged.

Instead of asking, *"Should I stop?"* try asking something more useful: *"What exactly is this doubt pointing to?"*

If you want to work with this practically, slow the moment down and reflect on the following:

- What specifically am I afraid might happen if I speak or decide here?
- Is this doubt about competence, or is it about potential consequences?
- What experience or insight do I already have that applies to this situation?
- If I didn't require certainty, what would my next move likely be?

Doubt becomes disruptive when it runs in the background unchecked, but it becomes manageable when you bring it into the open and examine it directly. You don't need to eliminate doubt in order to lead, but you need to learn how to act with it in the room.

And that's important because waiting for doubt to disappear is just another version of waiting for permission. And the goal isn't to silence uncertainty, it's to make sure it doesn't make your decisions for you.

5. Surround Yourself with Expansive People

Even when you've decided to stop waiting for permission, your environment still shapes how bold you feel. Some people expand your thinking and others quietly reinforce your hesitation. You've likely experienced both.

An expansive person doesn't flatter you or blindly agree. They also don't simply remove friction. What they do is different, they challenge your thinking without questioning your legitimacy, they ask you to go further instead of asking you to tone it down and they respond to your ideas as if they belong in the room.

Over time, these responses matter.

If the dominant voices around you constantly signal caution, risk and overanalysis, you'll naturally move more slowly. If the people around you treat initiative as normal and thoughtful risk as expected, you'll begin to mirror that instead.

So the question isn't just whether you have enough information to act, the question is whose reactions you're calibrating yourself against. To work with this practically, reflect on your current dynamics:

- When I share an early idea, who helps me develop it and who immediately pokes holes in it?
- Who asks me to clarify and sharpen my thinking, and who subtly signals that I should wait?
- In which conversations do I leave feeling clearer and more decisive?
- In which conversations do I leave feeling smaller or more doubtful than before?

Once you've answered those honestly, look for patterns. If you consistently feel more grounded after speaking with certain people, involve them earlier when you're shaping a decision. If you notice that a particular dynamic pushes you into overexplaining or reopening settled questions, experiment with shortening that loop. You might decide not to seek input from these people until you've already formed a clear direction and you might limit the discussion to specific questions instead of open ended validation seeking.

The goal isn't to eliminate disagreement, it's to become more intentional about whose voices shape your confidence. And that's important because leadership isn't built in isolation, it's reinforced, or undermined, by the people you regularly think out loud with.

Visual Summary

Practice	What It Looks Like	Why It Works
1. Build Inner Permission First	Deciding privately that your judgment counts. Not waiting for reassurance before speaking. Naming the permissions you're no longer waiting for and acting on them in real moments.	Breaks the habit of outsourcing legitimacy. Shifts authority from external validation to internal conviction. Reduces hesitation rooted in approval seeking.
2. Start Small, But Start Now	Speaking earlier than usual. Shortening the gap between thinking and acting. Offering a perspective before it's fully polished. Adjusting your timing deliberately.	Builds behavioral momentum. Rewires hesitation patterns. Strengthens confidence through repetition rather than intensity.
3. Practice Micro Visibility	Contributing regularly instead of rarely. Letting your voice appear more than once. Treating presence as normal rather than high stakes.	Normalizes visibility. Reduces the emotional charge around being seen. Makes contribution habitual instead of dramatic.
4. Reframe Self-Doubt as Data	Pausing to examine doubt instead of obeying it. Asking what fear is pointing to. Acting with uncertainty rather than waiting for certainty.	Prevents doubt from driving behavior. Increases discernment. Builds the ability to lead without requiring complete confidence.
5. Surround Yourself with Expansive People	Noticing who sharpens your thinking and who shrinks it. Involving people who encourage constructive dialogue. Limiting overvalidation loops.	Strengthens decisive behavior. Reduces environmental reinforcement of hesitation. Anchors authority in supportive dynamics rather than constant approval.

Micro-Practice: Decide Before You Ask

Once this week, catch the moment right before you reach for reassurance. It might be an email you're about to send, a point you're about to raise in a meeting, or a decision you're about to delay while you wait for one more opinion. Pause there, not to overthink it, but to notice what you're actually doing in real time.

Before you ask anyone else, ask yourself this one question first:

- Do I already have enough information to decide or move forward?

If the answer is yes, then move forward. Send the message, say the sentence, make the call.

Afterwards, take two minutes to reflect in writing:

- What happened when I decided without asking first?
- What did I learn about my own judgment in that moment?
- What felt uncomfortable, and what actually felt grounding?

This isn't about being right all the time, it's about interrupting the reflex to outsource your authority and building proof, week by week, that you can trust yourself to move.

Practical Quick Phrases

Hesitation often sneaks into your language. You soften your point, you over explain, you invite agreement before you've even finished your sentence. Having a few steady phrases ready can help you stay grounded in the moment and speak from ownership instead of from apology or from validation seeking.

These aren't about sounding certain, they're about sounding clear.

You might try:

- *"Here's what I'm seeing."*
- *"This feels important to me."*
- *"I'm going to suggest we move in this direction."*
- *"This is the decision I'm comfortable making."*
- *"I don't have full certainty, but I have enough to act."*
- *"Let's move and adjust if we need to."*

- *"I'm going to go first on this."*
- *"I see it differently, and here's why."*
- *"I'm comfortable standing behind this call."*
- *"We can keep discussing it, but at some point we need to decide."*

None of these claim perfection, but they claim responsibility. They signal that you're willing to step forward without waiting to be invited, while still staying open to learning and adjustment.

Checklist: What Will You Try This Week?

Change doesn't happen when you agree with an idea, it happens when you test it in a real moment. Use this checklist to choose one or two behaviors you're willing to practice this week, not perfectly, but intentionally.

- I'll write down one specific permission I'm no longer waiting for.
- I'll speak once before I feel fully ready.
- I'll make my voice visible in a small, repeatable way.
- I'll treat self-doubt as information instead of a stop sign.
- I'll make a decision without waiting for full agreement.

Closing: No One Is Coming

When I first started creating content about neurodiversity, introversion, grief, burnout and leadership, I was terrified. Not of writing itself, but of what it might cost me. I worried about credibility and I worried about how it would be perceived inside corporate spaces. Would this limit me? Would people take me less seriously? Would I be seen as too much or not enough?

For a long time, I edited myself for safety. I softened the language, I removed the sharper edges, I waited for signals that it was acceptable to go further and I waited for reassurance that I wouldn't pay a price for being honest.

As I waited, nothing changed. And slowly, that lack of change became louder than the fear. I realized that no one was going to tell me it was safe. No one was going to formally approve the version of me that wanted to speak about masking, love, exhaustion or ambition in professional spaces. If I was going to say those things, I would have to say them without a guarantee.

So I did. Not all at once, not dramatically, but gradually. I stopped writing as if someone else needed to approve my perspective first, I stopped framing my voice as a liability and something interesting happened. Each time I shared something that felt honest rather than strategic, someone would write to me and say, *"I thought I was the only one,"* or *"Thank you for saying this out loud."*

That's when I understood something I hadn't been able to see before: the permission I was waiting for wasn't something anyone else could have given me. And that's because it came after I acted, not before.

And this pattern isn't unique to me.

Reshma Saujani is a lawyer, activist and the founder of *Girls Who Code*, a nonprofit organization dedicated to closing the gender gap in technology. Before founding it, she left a successful legal career and decided to run for Congress in New York. She had no traditional political background, no long track record inside party structures and no clear signal that she was the *"right"* candidate. By most conventional standards, she didn't look ready.

She has written openly about how unqualified she felt when she first entered the race and how exposed it was to step into a space where she didn't fit the expected mold. She ran anyway and she lost. For a while, that loss felt like confirmation of every doubt she had carried. But during the campaign, she noticed something else. She met girls who had already internalized the belief that technology and leadership were not meant for them, not because of ability, but because no one had ever shown them that they belonged.

That realization became the foundation for *Girls Who Code*. What began as a response to defeat grew into a movement that has reached hundreds of thousands of students worldwide.[92] Her authority didn't come from winning or being endorsed, it emerged from acting before she felt fully ready and allowing the work itself to shape the next chapter.

Susan Cain's story carries a similar thread. For years, she absorbed the message that leadership required a louder personality and a different presence. Instead of continuing to adapt herself to fit that model, she wrote *Quiet* and challenged the assumption that extroversion was the default for influence. At the time, there was no guarantee that her argument would resonate, but it did. Her work reshaped how millions understand leadership and temperament, not because she matched the dominant style, but because she trusted her perspective enough to articulate it clearly.[1]

What connects these stories is not the scale of the success, but the sequence. Neither of them were tapped on the shoulder to be told it was their turn nor were either of them declared ready by a system that fully understood them. They moved before they felt certain, they acted before they received endorsement and in both cases legitimacy followed.

Most systems are slow to recognize non-traditional leadership. Instead they reward familiarity, they reward visible confidence and they reward what already looks like authority. If you wait to feel completely ready, completely confident or completely approved, you may end up waiting indefinitely.

No one is coming.

No one is going to confirm that you are qualified enough to speak the way you want to speak. No one is going to remove the doubt before you act. And no one is going to guarantee that stepping forward won't carry risk.

Leadership isn't granted when certainty arrives, it's claimed when you decide your judgment is sufficient to act.

That doesn't mean ignoring fear and it doesn't mean pretending you don't care what happens. It means recognizing that fear and doubt often show up precisely when something matters.

So stop waiting for someone to validate your ambition. Stop waiting for the perfect version of yourself. And stop waiting for the room to feel completely safe.

If you're already thinking deeply, taking responsibility, caring about the impact of your work and choosing integrity over performance, you're not preparing to lead.

You're already leading.

And no one is coming to tell you that it's allowed.

Rule 10: Lead Anyway

"We are the ones we have been waiting for"
June Jordan

By the time you reach this rule, you probably already feel what it's asking of you. Not because everything is clear or resolved, but because you've been carrying the tension for a long time. The tension between being effective and being yourself, between adapting just enough to succeed and wondering how much of yourself you're allowed to keep in that process.

This final rule isn't about becoming bolder or louder. Nor is it about finally feeling confident. That would go against everything I've written before. This final rule is about recognizing that leadership doesn't begin once you've resolved all of that tension, it actually begins while you're still in it.

I never thought of myself as someone who would challenge systems. I've been too much of a people pleaser throughout my life and I've cared far too much about what other people think of me to rebel in any obvious way. I wasn't the loudest in the room, I didn't march into meetings with a mission statement and I never wanted to overthrow anything. I wanted to do good work, blend in and hopefully do so without losing myself in the process.

Over the years, as I slowly allowed myself to be more who I am at work, something changed. It didn't happen fast nor dramatically, just slowly. I started wanting to be seen as I was and to lead without constantly shrinking myself to fit a mold I didn't fit in. And at some point, I realized that this was the change. Not a big rebellion, not a public stand, just the decision to be present as who I am, even when the room wasn't built for me and even when I couldn't see anyone like me in it.

And the more I allowed myself to show up honestly, the more I became aware of how much I had been adapting before.

In meetings and leadership offsites, I began noticing patterns I had normalized for years. I would sit among confident voices that seemed born to decide, and I would calculate the exact moment to speak so I wouldn't interrupt or take up too much space. I would edit myself in real time so I didn't sound messy, emotional, or too intense. I was constantly adjusting tone, speed, and wording. And I carried an exhaustion I couldn't fully name. Was it grief, was it masking or was it the quiet strain of trying to belong in systems that were never designed for people like me?

I thought about leaving many times. I thought about changing jobs, changing careers or walking away. Part of me was afraid of the unknown, and that fear kept me where I was. But another part of me, smaller and quieter, wanted to stay. Not to endure, not out of obligation, and certainly not because I enjoy suffering. I wanted to stay because I sensed that staying might actually change something.

We talk a lot about leaving. About walking away when something doesn't fit, about starting over and sometimes that's exactly the right decision. But we talk far less about staying. Not staying out of fear or resignation, but staying by choice. Staying with integrity and staying without disappearing.

That kind of staying rarely looks impressive. No one applauds it, there's no headline and most of the time it just feels slow and, if I'm honest, a little lonely. It can feel invisible, but when I look back, that's often where the real shifts happened. Not through dramatic exits or big declarations, but through people who kept showing up as themselves and refused to slowly disappear.

Hannah Gadsby built a career as a stand up comedian, an industry that rewards sharpness, emotional distance, and self deprecation. For years, she adapted herself to fit those expectations and she turned her own trauma into something the audience could laugh at. It worked, she was successful, but it came at a cost.

Gadsby has explained that the version of comedy she had learned required her to humiliate herself in order to be accepted. The joke worked because she made herself the punchline. Over time, she began to recognize what that pattern was doing and it trained her to make herself smaller so other people could stay comfortable. Instead of leaving comedy entirely, she chose to stay and change how she practiced it.

In *Nanette*, Gadsby explicitly breaks the traditional structure of stand up comedy. Instead of setting up tension and releasing it with a punchline, she refuses the release. Mid story, she stops and explains why the punchline itself is harmful. She does so as she recounts an assault by a man who mistook her for a gay man, then pauses to explain that the joke version of that story, which she had told on stage for years, relied on self deprecation and minimization to make the audience comfortable. In Nanette, she refuses to end with herself as the joke. That moment isn't comedy, it's exposure. By stopping the punchline, she shows the mechanics of how humour can soften violence and train people to accept it as normal.[92]

That, to me, is what leading anyway can look like. It's staying visible without making yourself smaller so others stay comfortable. It's telling the truth even when it would be easier to wrap it in something softer. And it's changing a space not by storming out of it, but by showing up differently inside it and refusing to perform a version of yourself that keeps the room at ease.

Whitney Wolfe Herd shows a different version of the same story. She started her career in tech in environments that were openly hostile to women. She was part of the founding team at *Tinder* and later experienced harassment and exclusion that pushed her to leave and pursue legal action. At that point, walking away from tech entirely would have made sense and most people would have done exactly that. Instead, she stayed.

She looked closely at how power actually worked in digital dating. Who made the first move, who set the tone and who carried the risk. And then she built something that shifted that dynamic. *Bumble* was structured around a simple change: women make the first move.

That wasn't a branding tweak. She changed one of the basic rules the dating industry had been built on. On most platforms, engagement is everything. More messages, more swipes, more activity. Growth is the goal while comfort and safety are secondary, if they're considered at all. By structuring *Bumble* so women make the first move, she shifted that assumption. That choice likely reduced certain types of engagement and it probably slowed things down, but it also increased a sense of control and psychological safety for women using the platform. She chose to prioritize this over standard performance.

She didn't wait for the tech world to become more equitable, she changed one of its core incentives and accepted that it might come at a cost.[93]

Those are the kinds of changes that resonate with me. They're not dramatic, they don't always trend, but they're honest, and they alter something at the root.

And that matters, because change doesn't have to look like a headline. It can look like a trans employee insisting on using their real pronouns at work or an introverted executive who stops performing extroversion just to be seen as competent or a woman of color who declines yet another diversity panel and decides where her energy actually belongs.

What if leading anyway isn't loud at all? What if it's already happening in small, deliberate acts that quietly reshape how we work and how we lead?

Lead from the Edges to Change the Center

Revolutions aren't always loud. Some begin quietly in small refusals, in subtle shifts or in moments when something that once felt acceptable no longer does.

In *The Power of the Powerless*, Václav Havel tells the story of a greengrocer living under a totalitarian regime in late twentieth century Czechoslovakia. Every day, the grocer places a political slogan in his shop window. He does so not because he believes in it, but because it's expected that he does so and because everyone else does it. And everyone does it because not doing so would draw attention. This is a ritual of compliance.

One day, the greengrocer removes the sign. Nothing else changes. He doesn't protest and he doesn't explain himself. He simply stops participating in something he no longer believes to be true. And yet, Havel argues, this small act is revolutionary. It's revolutionary not because it crumples the system overnight, but because it exposes the system's dependence on quiet compliance. The regime survives not through force alone, but through the everyday rituals people perform to avoid standing out.[94]

Decades later, the same story continues to resurface in very different forums. It was referenced by Mark Carney in a speech at the *World Economic Forum* in Davos 2026, not as a historical anecdote, but as a reminder that systems rarely change because of rebellion alone. They change when ordinary people stop participating in what they know is wrong.[95]

That is how many revolutions actually begin. They don't begin with force or spectacle, but with a decision to stop living a lie.

In many organizations, leadership has long been defined by conformity. Success is associated with editing yourself for acceptability, smoothing out what makes you different, and learning to behave like the people already in power. We're rewarded for adapting first and questioning later and we're asked to fit in before we're allowed to influence.

That model has produced leaders who look the same, sound the same, and solve problems the same way. It has also pushed many capable people to the margins or excluded them from leadership altogether. Not because they lack leadership ability, but because their way of thinking, communicating, or showing up doesn't match the dominant template.

If you've spent years masking who you are to survive in corporate environments, unmasking can feel dangerous. If you're introverted in a culture that equates confidence with volume, staying true to your style can feel like resistance. If you're neurodivergent in structures built for linear, predictable minds, asking for what you need can feel like asking for too much. But what if those experiences aren't signs that you don't belong? What if they're evidence that you see something others don't?

That experience, of being slightly outside while still inside, has been written about long before corporate leadership books existed.

Cultural theorist bell hooks writes about it in *Feminist Theory: From Margin to Center*. When she talks about the margin, she isn't romanticizing it, she's describing what it's like to live inside systems where you're the one adjusting.[96]

The margin is where you double check your tone before you speak. Where you study how others behave so you don't stand out in the wrong way. Where you notice which comments get praised and which ones make the room tense. Over time, living there, in the margin, makes you attentive. You learn to read patterns quickly and you see how power actually moves.

Hooks argues that this position creates a kind of clarity. From the edges, you notice what's missing because you're the one compensating for it. You see which behaviors are rewarded, which voices are interrupted and which leadership styles are quietly dismissed. Not because you're analyzing it from a distance, but because you've had to navigate it yourself.

This perspective from the margins isn't theoretical, it's practical. When you've lived on the margins, you don't speak about leadership in abstract models, you speak about what actually happens in real situations. You notice who gets interrupted, you notice who has to overprepare and you notice which ideas are heard only when repeated by someone else.

That kind of awareness changes how you lead. You don't rely only on frameworks or leadership policies, you rely on what you've observed, what you've experienced and what you've had to navigate yourself. And that perspective is something the center often lacks, because when you're comfortable inside a system, you don't always see how it excludes others.

That is why leading from the edges isn't a disadvantage, but it's a form of insight the system rarely values, but deeply needs.

And when you carry that perspective into leadership, you don't just adapt yourself to the existing path. You start questioning the path itself. You start asking whether the way things are done still makes sense, whether the expectations people quietly absorb are actually necessary and whether the norms everyone follows are actually working, or if they're just complied with.

And once you see that, you can't unsee it. You may still operate inside the system, but you're no longer quietly aligned with it. At some point, you stop adjusting yourself to fit it and begin adjusting it instead. And adjusting it doesn't always mean redesigning the whole structure. Often, it means changing how power is used in the environment you're already in. It means interrupting patterns, it means redistributing attention and it means refusing to dominate simply because you can.

Sometimes that shift doesn't look dramatic at all, it simply looks like a different way of leading. Research by Susan Cain shows that introverted leaders often build stronger teams, especially in environments where initiative and autonomy matter. Not because they dominate the room, but because they don't. They listen, they leave space, they don't rush to fill silence and in doing so, other people step forward.[1]

The same pattern shows up in research on neurodivergent talent. In the Harvard Business Review article *Neurodiversity as a Competitive Advantage*, organizations that actively include neurodivergent professionals outperform their peers in innovation and problem solving. Different cognitive styles interrupt groupthink as they question assumptions others have stopped noticing and they expose blind spots simply by thinking differently.[97]

In other words, the people who feel slightly out of place in traditional leadership structures often hold exactly the perspective those structures lack.

And that is the revolution this rule points to.

You don't need to tear everything down to be radical nor do you need to leave the system to change it. Change often begins when someone stays, but refuses to disappear. Change takes shape when people stop performing leadership in ways that cost them their integrity and it happens when they choose to lead anyway.

This can look like a manager who says, *"I don't have all the answers, but I'll create space for us to find them together."* This can also look like a senior leader who's openly autistic and stops masking in high stakes settings. And it can be as simple as someone who pushes back on hustle culture, not because they lack ambition, but because they want to build something sustainable.

These acts may not look revolutionary at first glance and they probably won't get any applause at the moment. But over time, they change what feels normal, they reshape norms, they shift what gets rewarded, they make room for people and they quietly signal that another way of leading is possible.

You don't need a platform to create impact and you don't need a megaphone to change a system. If you're leading from where you stand, as who you are, without adjusting yourself into invisibility, you're already participating in change.

And let's remember, the world doesn't need more leaders who fit the mold, it needs people willing to lead anyway.

Start Where You Are

We tend to imagine change as something big and public. We tend to see it as a moment that gets headlines or as a bold declaration or as a system redesigned overnight.

But most revolutions that actually last don't begin that way. They begin quietly, in the ordinary decisions we make about who we are willing to be when no one is applauding. They begin when you speak up in a meeting even though your voice shakes and you fear it's not your place to share your thoughts. They begin when you say no to a project, not because you're incapable, but because you're already at capacity. They begin when you show up to work as you are, quiet, autistic, introverted, observant or whoever you might be, and you stop apologizing for it.

These moments rarely look impressive from the outside. Speaking up in a meeting isn't regarded often as an accomplishment on its own, even if it can be. So while these moments might look mundane externally, on the inside, they often feel uncomfortable or even risky. And because these moments don't necessarily look like leadership as we have been taught to recognize it, they're easy to dismiss or ignore. But don't let that fool you. These moments accumulate and over time, they change how leadership is practiced. Not through force, but through consistency.

History is full of examples of this kind of change. Not the dramatic kind, but the slow, deliberate refusal to participate in something that no longer feels true.

Under authoritarian regimes, many of the changes that eventually mattered didn't begin with open protest. They began when ordinary people stopped playing along in small, quiet ways. Some civil servants continued doing their jobs, but they stopped adding the visible signs of loyalty that were expected, the slogans in windows, the public affirmations, the small rituals that signaled agreement. They followed the rules, but they no longer performed belief. On their own, these choices didn't look dramatic, but together, they weakened one of the system's core assumptions: that everyone supported it, that everyone agreed, that compliance was genuine.

A powerful example of this is Estonia's *Singing Revolution*. Over the course of more than a decade, Estonians gathered repeatedly to sing traditional folk songs and hymns that had been discouraged or banned under Soviet rule. These gatherings weren't framed as protests, they looked cultural and almost harmless. Just people showing up and singing.

People came together night after night, year after year, to sing in their own language, to remember their history out loud, and to affirm an identity the regime had tried to suppress. There were no speeches, no clear demands, instead, all there was was presence, repetition, and refusal to let go of what mattered. For a long time, nothing seemed to happen.

And then, slowly, it did.

By the late 1980s, these acts of cultural persistence had become a mass movement. In 1991, Estonia regained its independence. The revolution didn't succeed because of a single decisive moment, but because people stayed, they kept showing up, they refused to perform loyalty, and they refused to disappear.[98]

That's what a quiet revolution looks like. It's not urgency or spectacle, but endurance. It's a long commitment to what we believe to be true that eventually reshapes what's possible.

That same dynamic also exists in organizations.

When I first became a leader, I assumed there was a version of leadership I needed to live up to. I believed I needed to be upbeat, I needed to be fast and to be visible everywhere. I believed I needed to perform confidence at all times and I tried to lead that way for longer than I should have. Not only was it hard because it wasn't me, but it cost me more than I realized.

I was exhausted from trying to be someone else at work and I feared people would believe my exhaustion came from the role being too big for me. That wasn't the case. The role wasn't too big, but the exhaustion came from the performance that was unsustainable. During that period, I spent a large portion of my energy monitoring my tone, my facial expressions, and my presence in rooms that were already loud enough without me trying to match them.

My personal shift didn't happen all at once and it wasn't a decision I announced. It happened slowly, as I allowed myself to lead in a way that felt more natural to me and allowed myself to be calmer, more deliberate, openly neurodivergent and more focused on clarity than charisma.

And over time something changed. People didn't disengage, although some might have, as I didn't fit the mold they expected me to embrace, but most people leaned in. I believe they did so not because I became louder or more inspiring, but because I stopped hiding and started showing who I actually was. And in doing that, I wasn't just leading differently, I was modeling a version of leadership that many people recognized but hadn't seen before. Something calmer, more deliberate and more human. Trust grew, not because I performed confidence better, but because performance was replaced with clarity and authenticity. And trust grows faster when leadership feels real rather than rehearsed.

I saw the changes here and there in small moments. In meetings where others spoke more freely, when team members admitted uncertainty earlier on and more openly and when decisions improved because fewer people were pretending to agree when they didn't. None of it was dramatic or happened with fireworks, but all the small changes took place and they mattered.

This is when I realized something important, authenticity isn't the opposite of professionalism, it's the foundation of it.

Leadership researcher Amy Edmondson has shown that trust and psychological safety don't emerge from certainty or perfection, but from leaders who are willing to be honest, admit limits, and create space for others to contribute. When leaders stop performing invulnerability, teams don't lose confidence in their leadership, instead they gain it. [38]

As leaders, we're not here to become more acceptable versions of ourselves. We're here to create space for others, but also for ourselves. When you stop shrinking to fit a mold that was never designed for you, you expand what leadership and professionalism can look like.

That expansion rarely happens through formal authority or announcements. It happens through example, through what you model day after day, often without realizing it. And whether you realize it or not, people are always watching. They watch how you respond to pressure, they notice what you tolerate and they see whether you stay silent or whether you speak truthfully.

This is where representation begins to matter. Not as symbolism, but as example.

Representation isn't only about visibility, it's also about permission. Every time someone sees you lead without performing, without apologizing for who you are, without sanding yourself down to be acceptable, you give others permission to do the same. And that's how cultures shift. They don't change when someone announces a new value, but when someone lives it consistently enough that others feel safe to follow.

Albert Bandura wrote, *"Most human behavior is learned observationally through modeling."* [99] Leadership is learned the same way. People don't learn how to lead from what we say we value, but they learn it from what we model, tolerate, and repeat. They learn from how we show up under pressure, from whether we stay present or disappear and from whether we choose honesty over performance, and consistency over approval.

You don't have to change everything at once and you don't have to announce a new way of leading. You can start exactly where you are, with the next meeting, the next decision, the next moment where you choose to stay visible rather than shrink.

That is how quiet revolutions begin and that's how leadership changes, one example at a time. You already see what doesn't work and you already know what it costs to keep shrinking, so lead anyway.

Tips and Tools: Staying and Leading Anyway

Leading anyway doesn't mean pushing harder, becoming louder, or forcing visible change. Leading anyway means staying present, staying honest, and staying aligned, even when the system wasn't built for you or it's uncomfortable.

1. Notice Where You Shrink and Stay With It

There are moments at work when you can feel yourself adjusting in real time, not because anyone explicitly asked you to, but because something in the room signals that it might be easier if you did. You're about to make a point and you soften it before it fully forms, you have a question but decide it's safer to let it pass, or you translate what you actually think into something more neutral and less likely to create friction. It happens quickly, often so quickly that you barely notice it, and over time that adjustment becomes automatic.

Gradually, you begin assuming that you are the variable that needs to shift. If the tone feels tense, you smooth it. If the direction feels misaligned, you double check yourself first. If something feels uncomfortable, you interpret that discomfort as a sign that you should recalibrate rather than as information about the environment you're in. This isn't a personal flaw and it isn't a weakness. Many of us learned early to read rooms carefully because it was necessary. We learned what was rewarded, what was tolerated, and what quietly created resistance, and we adapted accordingly.

Rule 10 doesn't ask you to stop doing this overnight, but it asks you to start noticing it. Pay attention to the moments where you soften a point until it barely resembles what you meant, or where you decide not to speak at all because it feels safer. These moments aren't failures, they reveal where the system quietly pressures you to disappear.

French philosopher Michel Foucault wrote extensively about how power operates not primarily through force, but through internalization. Over time, people begin to regulate themselves, they anticipate what will be accepted and they correct themselves in advance. No one needs to silence them, because they do it themselves. [100]

That is what shrinking often looks like in organizations. It doesn't look like censorship, but simple self-regulation.

Here is one way to stay present in those moments, without making a scene or forcing change you're not ready for: When you notice yourself shrinking, slow down enough to register it and notice what made you hesitate. You don't need to change your behavior and you don't need to correct yourself. Simply noticing is enough to start as it interrupts the automatic nature of the response.

This kind of awareness doesn't immediately lead to confidence or action. Often it leads to uncertainty and that's completely fine. The work at this stage isn't to speak more, but to disappear less.

Over time, this awareness creates space. Not space to become louder, but space to choose. You may still soften your point and you may still decide the moment isn't right, but now it is a decision rather than a reflex. And when something becomes a decision, it belongs to you again.

2. Define Success in Language That Fits You

If success is measured only by visibility, speed, or dominance, many forms of leadership will always look like failure. Those measures aren't neutral, they're inherited from systems that reward conformity and reproduction of what already exists. When those are the only metrics that count, quieter, slower, or more deliberate styles can easily look like underperformance, even when they are creating stability, clarity, and long-term results.

Rule 10 asks you to redefine success in a way that reflects the impact you actually want to have, not the behavior the system has historically rewarded. This is not about lowering standards, it's about choosing standards that align with your values, your nervous system, and the kind of culture you want to build.

If you don't define success for yourself, you will inherit a definition by default. And inherited definitions often reward the most visible contribution rather than the most meaningful one. They reward speaking often rather than thinking carefully and urgency rather than sustainability. When you measure yourself only through that lens, you risk dismissing the very strengths that make your leadership effective.

Redefining success begins privately. It begins by asking yourself what actually matters to you when you are leading well.

You might reflect on questions like:

- When I leave a meeting feeling satisfied, what actually happened?
- What tells me I have led well, even if no one explicitly praises it?
- What kind of environment do I create when I am at my best?
- Which outcomes matter to me, even if they are not the loudest or most visible?
- Where am I chasing comparison instead of impact?

When comparison shows up, as it inevitably will, remind yourself that different leadership styles are not competing for the same prize, they are solving different problems. A leader who stabilizes a team during uncertainty is not competing with a leader who energizes a large audience, they are doing different work.

Defining success in a way that fits you doesn't mean withdrawing from high standards, it means choosing standards you can sustain without shrinking yourself to meet them. And once you become clear about what you are actually aiming for, it becomes much harder for external metrics to quietly pull you away from yourself.

3. Treat Your Difference as Information, Not a Limitation

Many of us have been taught that our differences, whether that's introversion, a different way of thinking, social style, or something less visible, are problems to manage. Something to soften, to hide, or to compensate for. Over time, that framing becomes internal and you stop trusting yourself. Instead of leading from who you are, you focus on fitting in as well as you can.

Rule 10 invites us to shift our mindset. Instead of treating your difference as something to work around, hide, soften or compensate for, it asks you to treat it as information.

Your lived experience shapes how you notice risk, how you read dynamics, and how you understand impact. If you're introverted, you may notice when conversations are moving too fast for real thinking to happen. If you're neurodivergent, you may spot patterns, inconsistencies, or inefficiencies others overlook. If you've lived on the margins, you often sense early when decisions will land badly for people who aren't in the room.

These aren't just personality traits, they are forms of perception and perception is part of leadership.

bell hooks wrote about how living at the margins creates a different relationship to power. You don't experience systems as abstract ideas, you experience them through their consequences. Policies aren't concepts, they are lived realities. Decisions aren't neutral, they land somewhere and on someone. When you're isolated from the consequences of the decisions that are made, it becomes easier to misunderstand risk, minimize harm, or believe that systems are working because they appear orderly from the center.

You see this dynamic clearly in fiction as well. In *The Hunger Games*, life in the Capitol is comfortable and disconnected. Those in power can't truly imagine what life is like in the districts, not because they're cruel, but because they're in the center and they're far removed from the cost of the system that benefits them.[101]

Living closer to the edges changes perspectives, it sharpens perception and it makes it harder to ignore what's missing, who's excluded, and which norms quietly shape behavior. What feels theoretical at the center becomes concrete at the margins.

In environments that reward alignment with the center, this kind of perception isn't always welcomed. Over time, leaders who see these patterns can start to mistrust their own observations, they second-guess what they notice and they might assume they are overreacting or being too sensitive.

That is often the moment where difference turns from insight into self-doubt. You can interrupt that shift by asking yourself:

- What do I tend to notice early that others only recognize once it becomes a problem?
- Which decisions make me uneasy even when they are widely supported, and what might that unease be pointing to?
- When I rush to keep up, what part of my thinking gets lost?
- Where do I hold back a concern because everyone else seems aligned?
- What happens when I don't voice the doubt I felt early on?
- What do I notice that no one else is naming?
- What patterns do I see that others seem to accept as normal?

Treating your difference as information doesn't mean turning it into an identity statement or constantly explaining yourself. It means allowing that perspective to inform your judgment, your priorities, and the questions you are willing to raise. It means trusting that what you notice is not automatically a flaw to correct, but often a signal worth examining.

4. Make Small Cultural Shifts Explicit

Culture doesn't change through values statements or town halls, it changes through what's repeated, tolerated, and left unchallenged in everyday interactions.

Most people learn what's acceptable at work not from official policies, but from watching what leaders do when something uncomfortable happens. We learn from seeing who gets interrupted, who's protected, what's rushed, what's named, and what's ignored.

Rule 10 isn't about fixing culture in one move. Changing a culture can never be done overnight. Rule 10 is about staying present long enough for your behavior to become a reference point and part of the change.

When you model boundaries, honesty, or care, you're not making a point, you're teaching. These moments may feel small, especially when they don't come with recognition or immediate results, but they're visible, and over time, they accumulate into norms.

One way to stay grounded in this kind of leadership is to make your actions clear enough that others can understand and repeat them. It's important that your actions aren't performance, but honest so they can become a signal of something different. This, at times, can even mean to name what you're doing out loud, not to draw attention to yourself, but to remove uncertainty about what's acceptable.

That can look like being the leader who leaves the office at a reasonable hour and doesn't apologize for it or choosing not to reply to emails late at night, even when you technically could. It can mean saying, *"I'll pick this up tomorrow"* instead of performing urgency.

These actions are simple, but they are noticeable. Over time, they make it clear that rest, boundaries, and sustainability aren't exceptions, they're part of how you work.

5. Speak Truth in Proportion to Your Capacity

Speaking honestly doesn't require speeches, declarations, or dramatic moments, what it requires is consistency.

Rule 10 isn't an invitation to say everything, everywhere, all at once. That kind of honesty often burns people out or puts them at risk. Leading anyway means choosing to be honest and truthful in ways that you can sustain, and that fit both your energy and your context.

This is especially important if you have learned, consciously or not, that visibility comes at a cost. If you have spent years masking, softening your tone, holding back parts of yourself, or staying quiet to remain safe, you don't suddenly flip a switch and become fully exposed. Honesty has to match your capacity and it has to feel steady enough that you can repeat it.

Speaking truth in proportion to your capacity means choosing what to say, where to say it, and how often, without turning yourself into a spokesperson or a symbol. It means understanding that visibility isn't binary and that there are many ways to be present without being exposed.

Here are some questions you can use to decide where and how to speak truthfully without overwhelming yourself:

- Where does it feel safe enough to stop editing myself?

- In which conversation am I already tired of holding back?
- What have I been meaning to say for a while?
- What would feel relieving to say out loud?
- Where would one honest sentence actually change something?
- Which conversations drain me because I am constantly editing myself?

You don't need to raise every issue and you don't need to educate everyone. Often, speaking truth looks like naming a boundary, correcting an assumption, or allowing silence instead of filling it with reassurance. Quiet honesty, practiced over time, tends to travel further than dramatic statements that can't be sustained.

Visual Summary

Practice	What It Looks Like	Why It Works
1. Notice Where You Shrink and Stay With It	Catching yourself softening a point, holding back a question, or translating your thinking to make it more acceptable. Slowing down just enough to notice the reflex instead of immediately correcting yourself.	Awareness interrupts automatic self-editing. When shrinking becomes a choice rather than a reflex, you regain agency and reduce the quiet erosion of self-trust.
2. Define Success in Language That Fits You	Measuring your leadership by clarity, stability, trust, or long term impact instead of visibility, speed, or dominance. Privately redefining what "good leadership" means for you.	Self defined standards prevent you from chasing inherited metrics that reward performance over impact. Clear internal measures reduce comparison and strengthen alignment.

3. Treat Your Difference as Information, Not a Limitation	Trusting what you notice early. Naming unease instead of dismissing it. Allowing your perspective to inform your questions and decisions rather than filtering it out.	Marginal or different perspectives often detect risk, blind spots, and cultural tension sooner. Treating difference as insight increases perceptual depth and strategic awareness.
4. Make Small Cultural Shifts Explicit	Modeling boundaries, honesty, and sustainability in visible ways. Leaving on time. Naming priorities. Demonstrating care in ordinary moments.	Culture shifts through repetition and modeling. Visible behavior becomes a reference point that others can repeat, gradually reshaping norms.
5. Speak Truth in Proportion to Your Capacity	Choosing one honest sentence instead of a speech. Speaking where it feels steady enough to repeat. Allowing silence rather than over reassuring.	Sustainable honesty builds credibility and trust. Proportional truth telling prevents burnout while still shifting conversations and expectations over time.

Micro-Practice: Stay Present Without Performing

Choose one recurring moment where you usually shrink, rush, or over adjust who you are and how you behave. This could be a meeting, when you make decisions, when there's a disagreement or any situation where you notice yourself editing your tone, your words, or your presence.

For one week, practice the following:

Before the moment, remind yourself silently: *"I don't need to disappear or soften myself to be here."*

During the moment, do one small thing differently without explanation. This could be to pause a few extra seconds before responding, it might mean saying something closer to what you actually think or it could be to ask a difficult or uncomfortable question instead of smoothing things over. You don't need to try to make it impressive, choose something that feels slightly uncomfortable, but still manageable.

After the moment, notice the outcome. Don't do this in terms of approvals but in terms of costs. Ask yourself:

- Did this take more or less energy than performing?
- Did clarity increase or decrease?
- Did I feel more or less like myself afterwards?
- What changes when I don't over edit myself?

Repeat this in the same type of situation over the course of a week and observe what shifts. Not necessarily around you, but within you. That is often where the real change begins.

Practical Quick Phrases

These aren't scripts, but they're anchors to help you lead anyway and be yourself more easily in hard moments. Use them as written or adapt them to sound like you.

To stay present without performing

- *"I need a moment to think before responding."*
- *"Let me say this more directly."*
- *"I don't have a polished answer, but here's what I think."*

To resist smoothing things over

- *"I don't fully agree, and here's why."*
- *"That sounds aligned on the surface, but I'm not convinced it works."*
- *"Can we slow this down before we move on?"*

To hold your ground quietly

- *"I don't need to decide this right now."*
- *"I'm standing by what I said."*
- *"Let's sit with the discomfort for a moment."*
- *"I might be wrong, but this doesn't sit right with me."*

To make a different norm visible

- *"I'm logging off now. I'll pick this up tomorrow."*
- *"I'll come back with a clearer answer rather than a fast one."*
- *"I don't need consensus to move forward, just clarity."*

Checklist: What Will You Try This Week?

Leading anyway doesn't start with a grand gesture, it starts with one deliberate choice. Choose where you will practice staying visible this week.

- I'll pay attention to one moment where I start shrinking.
- I'll stay in one uncomfortable moment instead of smoothing it over.
- I'll say one thing more directly than I usually would.
- I'll model one boundary or behavior I want others to feel allowed to practice.
- I'll leave one interaction feeling more like myself than when I walked in.

Closing: We've Always Been the Revolution

You don't need a title to lead, you don't need a stage to be heard, and you don't need permission to change the systems you're working in, especially when those systems were never designed for you.

For a long time, I believed leadership worked with a delay. I believed that if I proved myself first by being efficient, agreeable, reliable, and easy to work with, then maybe one day I'd earn the right to ask for what I needed. Maybe then I could speak more honestly, maybe then I could stop translating myself and maybe then I could take up space without apology.

What I learned over time instead is that the cost of waiting was higher than the risk of showing up.

When I began to lead as myself, autistic, introverted, careful, present, something shifted. I wasn't more impressive, I wasn't louder and I surely wasn't more polished. To the contrary. But instead, I became clearer, more grounded and more consistent. And over time, that consistency built trust in a way that masking and performance could never have.

It didn't make everyone comfortable as no one is for everyone, but it made the right people feel safe. And leadership has always worked this way, even if we pretend otherwise.

Rosa Parks is often remembered as a tired woman who refused to give up her seat on a bus. That version sadly flattens the truth. Parks had been organizing, training, and resisting segregation for years before the day where she refused to give up her seat. And when she did so, she understood the risks of her refusal and she also knew the system depended on her compliance to keep functioning. When she stayed seated, she didn't argue or explain herself, she simply withdrew her consent. That quiet refusal exposed how fragile the system really was and her power wasn't in spectacle or confrontation, but in presence and persistence.[102]

Malala Yousafzai was targeted because she spoke publicly about girls' right to education in Pakistan. After surviving an assassination attempt at fifteen, she could have disappeared from public life and I'm sure many people would have understood if she had. Instead, she stayed visible in a way that was measured and deliberate. She continued speaking about education, not with rage or provocation, but with clarity, consistency, and moral steadiness. Over time, that steadiness shifted a global conversation and forced institutions to listen. Her leadership didn't come from volume, but from refusing to retreat.[103]

Susan Cain encountered a different kind of resistance. In cultures that equate leadership with charisma and dominance, introversion was treated as a flaw to overcome. Cain didn't try to become louder to be taken seriously. Instead, she wrote Quiet and reframed the narrative instead. By grounding her argument in research and lived experience, she stayed with her truth long enough for millions of people to recognize themselves in it. She didn't ask introverts to adapt to the system, she asked the system to expand.[1]

What these women have in common is that none of them waited to be invited and none of them asked whether the system was ready for the change they wanted to see. Instead, all of them, in their own ways, led anyway.

And this is what this rule (Rule 10: Lead Anyway) has been pointing to all along. If you've ever felt like you needed to tone yourself down to belong, that experience isn't a weakness, it's information. If you've ever felt exhausted from adapting, that exhaustion isn't a personal failure, it's a signal that the system might need to change.

Leadership doesn't begin when you resolve your doubts, it begins when you decide not to disappear because of them. It begins when you stay present, when you stop editing yourself into something smaller, when you choose clarity over performance and when you model the kind of leadership you wish you'd been offered.

This is how cultures change. They don't change through declarations, but through repeated examples. They don't change through permission, but through repetition.

You were never missing a credential.
You were never behind.
You were never meant to fit in to begin with.
You've always been the revolution.

Lead anyway.

Conclusion to Part 3: Changing the Game

For a long time, we were taught that leadership is a race. We have been told that leaders should be fast, certain and visible and that the goal is to arrive early. We have been trained to believe that to lead, we need to climb fast and stay polished enough to belong so we can be chosen.

But what Rules 8, 9, and 10 have been quietly revealing together is something else entirely.

Rule 8 reminded us that there's no expiration date on success. Life doesn't unfold in a straight line, and leadership doesn't expire if it comes later, or differently, or with pauses for healing, caregiving, or change. Detours aren't delays, they're part of the story, often the richest parts, and they teach us resilience, perspective, and depth that a straight-line career can't provide.

Rule 9 challenged us to stop waiting for permission. Permission rarely comes, and when it does, it often arrives too late. Real leadership is claimed in the moment, in small and brave acts of visibility. It's speaking up even when your voice shakes, it's sharing an idea even when you fear it's not perfect and it's naming your needs even when you've been taught to hide them. Progress doesn't begin with a promotion, it begins in micro-moments, in rooms where no one expects you to claim authority and when you do anyway.

Rule 10 showed us that authenticity, showing up as we are, without shrinking or performing, is itself a revolution. In cultures that reward sameness and silence, every act of honesty becomes a disruption. Every time you hold your boundaries, speak your truth, or refuse to contort yourself to belong, you expand what leadership can look like and you make space for others to do the same.

Together, these rules remind us that changing the game doesn't always mean tearing it down. In some cases it means quietly refusing to play by timelines that were never ours, in others it means naming our worth without waiting for approval. And sometimes it means leading from the edges until the center shifts. Culture doesn't change overnight, but it shifts every time one person chooses to lead differently and refuses to apologize for it.

Consider Taylor Swift, not as a pop star icon, but as a case study in structural change. Early in her career, she signed contracts that gave record labels ownership of her master recordings, a common practice in the music industry and one that leaves artists with little control over their own work. Years later, when those masters were sold without her consent, she faced a choice many artists before her had accepted as inevitable.

Instead of fighting quietly behind the scenes or moving on, she chose a different path. She re-recorded her early albums in full and released them again, reclaiming ownership of her songs by creating parallel versions she controlled and that she labelled Taylor's Version. This had not been done before and it was a patient, methodical move rather than a dramatic protest. But it fundamentally challenged long held assumptions about who holds power in creative industries and what artists are allowed to question.

When she decided to do so, she didn't know if her fans would buy her re-recordings and she didn't wait for the industry's approval. In other words, she didn't ask permission to rewrite the rules. And in doing so, she shifted the balance of power, not only for herself, but for other artists who suddenly saw a different option where none had seemed possible before. Cultural change often begins this way, not with rebellion for its own sake, but with one person deciding to act for what they believe in and staying with that decision long enough for others to follow.[104]

Leadership isn't about fitting into old definitions, it's about expanding them. It's about leaving a trail that others can follow without having to contort themselves to belong. Your presence, your perspective, your pace, all of it matters.

You don't need to be younger, louder, faster, or more polished. You don't need to wait for a signal that you're ready. You're already enough and the way you lead, nonlinear, boundary-setting, grief-carrying, unmasked, unapologetic is proof that another way is possible.

This is not just personal growth, it's a cultural change. Every time you choose to lead on your terms, you're not only rewriting your own story, you're rewriting what leadership can mean for everyone watching. And when enough of us do it, leadership itself is transformed from something exclusive and rigid into something expansive, human, and sustainable.

LEADERSHIP ON YOUR TERMS

A Manifesto for Those Who Lead When They Break the Mold

You don't have to fit the mold to be a leader.
You don't have to become louder, faster, or harder to be taken seriously.
You don't have to wait for permission to show up fully.

You're not too sensitive.
You're not too slow.
You're not too quiet.
You're not too much.
And you're not missing anything.

Your lived experience isn't a limitation.
It's information.
It's pattern recognition.
It's insight shaped by what you've had to navigate, adapt to, and survive.

Your differences aren't weaknesses.
They're how leadership changes.

You can lead without the performance.
You can lead without the shrinking.
You can lead without translating yourself.
You can lead without becoming someone else.

You can lead with calm.
You can lead with clarity.
You can lead with questions instead of certainty.
You can lead by listening, by thinking deeply, by caring in ways that don't always make noise.

You're allowed to set boundaries.
You're allowed to rest.
You're allowed to grieve and still lead.
You're allowed to stop performing professionalism at the cost of your health.

If you've ever been told you weren't leadership material
because you didn't fit the mold, follow the timeline, or play the part,
let this be your beginning.
Let this be your answer.
Let this be your refusal.

We lead with intention.
We lead with integrity.
We lead when we break the mold.
And we lead anyway.

EPILOGUE

You're not too quiet, you're not too late and you're not alone.

If you've made it this far, thank you.

Maybe you recognized yourself in these pages. Maybe you're the quiet achiever, the overthinker, the one who masks to survive, the one who doubts even when things are going well or the one who lies awake at night wondering if they're too much or not enough. If you're any of these people or all of them, I wrote this book for you. And for me.

For a long time, I tried to fit into a mold that was never designed for someone like me. I was told I was too intense, too emotional, too analytical, too quiet, too honest. And in between the lines I felt too neurodivergent, too queer and often too human. I learned to adapt, to soften, to perform and to survive. And for a while, it worked very well, but overtime it came at a cost.

What I've come to believe, slowly and often painfully, is this: you don't have to lead like anyone else to lead well, and you don't need fixing because there's nothing wrong with you.

You're not broken for needing more recovery time, you're not falling behind because you don't want to hustle nonstop, you're not a bad leader because you prefer listening over speaking and you're not failing because you're still figuring things out. Leadership, real leadership, isn't about perfection, it's about presence. And that's what matters most. It's about showing up even when your hands are shaking, it's about standing for something even when your voice is low and it's about staying human in systems that often ask you to be something else entirely.

When I first started speaking up and creating content online about these experiences, I didn't know if any of it would resonate. I assumed I might be naming things that were too specific, too personal, or too niche. I thought I might be the only one trying to lead from the inside while feeling like an outsider. But the more openly I spoke about masking, grief, imposter syndrome and being the quiet one in loud rooms, the more messages I received: *"Me too", "I thought I was the only one", "I didn't know you could lead like that."*

Those messages showed me something I hadn't fully understood before. The problem was never that we were failing at leadership, it was that many of us were trying to lead inside systems that had no language for who we were. We weren't behind, we weren't broken, instead we were navigating environments that rewarded performance over presence and certainty over honesty. And the moment someone named that out loud, others recognized themselves in it.

If you recognized yourself anywhere in this book, that's not an accident. It means you've been carrying questions that deserved better answers, it means you've been leading in ways that didn't always get named or rewarded, but still mattered. And it means you're not alone in feeling the tension between who you are and what leadership has been told to look like.

Whether you're autistic or introverted, grieving or burned out, starting over at fifty or stepping into leadership for the first time at twenty five, you belong here. You don't need to become louder, tougher, or faster. You don't need to prove your worth through exhaustion and you don't need to earn the right to be yourself. You've already earned your place simply by caring, by trying, and by getting back up when life knocked you down.

I didn't write this book because I've all the answers, I wrote it because I've lived through all these questions myself and that fear of not fitting in. I've had days where anxiety made it hard to breathe before a presentation, nights spent replaying decisions I had already made and mornings where I cried on my way to work. But it's not all bad, I've also had moments of clarity, moments where honesty created trust and moments where someone else felt safer because I stopped performing.

That is the kind of leadership the world needs more of. The kind that makes space, the kind that doesn't conform and the kind that leads anyway.

You're not too quiet, you're not too late, you're not too different and you're not behind. What you need is space. Space to lead with presence instead of performance, space to speak in your own way, at your own time and space to stop pretending you've it all figured out.

This is not a book about confidence, it's a book about courage. It's about choosing to lead when the system wasn't built for you, it's about trusting that your questions matter, that your limits matter, that your rest matters, and that your voice matters.

Leadership isn't a personality contest, it's a commitment to care.

Let me finish by telling you this: you're building something real, something honest and something different. Keep going, we need you. Because the future of leadership isn't more of the same, it's not louder, it's braver and it already looks a lot like you.

Lead anyway.

Laurence

BIBLIOGRAPHY

1. Cain S. Quiet: The Power of Introverts in a World That Can't Stop Talking. New York, NY: Crown Publishing Group; 2012.
2. Nadella S. Hit Refresh: The Quest to Rediscover Microsoft's Soul and Imagine a Better Future for Everyone. New York, NY: Harper Business; 2017.
3. Grant A, Gino F, Hofmann DA. The Hidden Advantages of Quiet Bosses. Harvard Business Review [Internet]. 2010 Dec. Available from: https://hbr.org/2010/12/the-hidden-advantages-of-quiet-bosses
4. Cuddy A. Presence: Bringing Your Boldest Self to Your Biggest Challenges. New York, NY: Little, Brown Spark; 2015.
5. Hedges K. The Power of Presence: Unlock Your Potential to Influence and Engage Others. New York, NY: AMACOM; 2017.
6. Bandura A. Self-Efficacy: the Exercise of Control. New York, NY: W H Freeman; 1997.
7. Scott K. Radical Candor: Be a Kick-Ass Boss Without Losing Your Humanity. New York, NY: St. Martin's Press; 2017.
8. Barrett LF. How Emotions Are Made: The Secret Life of the Brain. Boston, MA: Mariner Books; 2017.
9. Kline N. Time to Think: Listening to Ignite the Human Mind. London, UK: Cassell Illustrated; 1999.
10. Pentland A. The New Science of Building Great Teams. Harvard Business Review [Internet]. 2012 Apr. Available from: https://hbr.org/2012/04/the-new-science-of-building-great-teams
11. Schein EH. Humble Inquiry: The Gentle Art of Asking Instead of Telling. 2nd ed. Oakland, CA: Berrett-Koehler Publishers; 2021.
12. Frei F, Morriss A. Unleashed: The Unapologetic Leader's Guide to Empowering Everyone Around You. Boston, MA: Harvard Business Review Press; 2020.
13. Chamorro-Premuzic T. Why Do So Many Incompetent Men Become Leaders? (and How to Fix It). Boston, MA: Harvard Business Review Press; 2019.

14. Price D. Unmasking Autism: Discovering the New Faces of Neurodiversity. New York, NY: Harmony; 2022.

15. Cooper M. Cut Adrift: Families in Insecure Times. Berkeley, CA: University of California Press; 2014.

16. Kaufman SB, Gregoire C. Wired to Create: Unraveling the Mysteries of the Creative Mind. New York, NY: Perigee; 2015.

17. Page SE. The Diversity Bonus: How Great Teams Pay Off in the Knowledge Economy. Princeton, NJ: Princeton University Press; 2017.

18. Fricker M. Epistemic Injustice: Power and the Ethics of Knowing. Oxford, UK: Oxford University Press; 2007.

19. Goffman E. The Presentation of Self in Everyday Life. New York, NY: Anchor Books; 1959.

20. Hochschild AR. The Managed Heart: Commercialization of Human Feeling. Berkeley, CA: University of California Press; 1983.

21. Maté G. When the Body Says No: The Cost of Hidden Stress. Toronto, Canada: Vintage Canada; 2004.

22. Grant A. Originals: How Non-Conformists Move the World. New York, NY: Viking; 2016.

23. Brene B. Braving the Wilderness: The Quest for True Belonging and the Courage to Stand Alone. New York, NY: Random House; 2017.

24. Jacinda Ardern. A Different Kind of Power. Wellington, NZ: Harper Collins; 2024.

25. Berger JG. Changing on the Job: Developing Leaders for a Complex World. Stanford, CA: Stanford University Press; 2012.

26. Clance, Pauline R., Imes SA. The Impostor Phenomenon in High Achieving Women: Dynamics and Therapeutic Intervention. Psychotherapy: Theory, Research & Practice. 1978;15(3):241–7. doi:10.1037/h0086006

27. Bravata D, et al. Prevalence, Predictors, and Treatment of Impostor Syndrome: a Systematic Review. Journal of General Internal Medicine. 2020;35(4):1252–75.

28. Heifetz RA, Grashow A, Linsky M. The Practice of Adaptive Leadership: Tools and Tactics for Changing Your Organization and the World. Boston, MA: Harvard Business Press; 2009.

29. Brown B. Daring Greatly: How the Courage to Be Vulnerable Transforms the Way We Live, Love, Parent, and Lead. New York, NY: Gotham Books; 2012.
30. Paquette L. Corporate Life: I Don't Always Know What I'm Doing. Blog - laurencepaquette.com [Internet]. 2023. Available from: https://www.laurencepaquette.com/post/corporate-life-i-dont-always-know-what-im-doing
31. Young V. The Secret Thoughts of Successful Women: Why Capable People Suffer from the Impostor Syndrome and How to Thrive in Spite of It. New York, NY: Crown Business; 2011.
32. Neff K. Self-Compassion: The Proven Power of Being Kind to Yourself. New York, NY: William Morrow; 2011.
33. Seligman MEP. Flourish: A Visionary New Understanding of Happiness and Well-being. New York, NY: Free Press; 2011.
34. Heifetz RA, Linsky M. Leadership on the Line: Staying Alive Through the Dangers of Leading. Boston, MA: Harvard Business School Press; 2002.
35. David S. Emotional Agility: Get Unstuck, Embrace Change, and Thrive in Work and Life. New York, NY: Avery; 2016.
36. Brown B. Dare to Lead: Brave Work. Tough Conversations. Whole Hearts. New York, NY: Random House; 2018.
37. Alison Wood Brooks, Maurice E. Schweitzer, Nicholas Epley. It Doesn't Hurt to Ask: Question-Asking Increases Liking. Journal of Personality and Social Psychology. 2017;113(3):430–52.
38. Edmondson AC. The Fearless Organization: Creating Psychological Safety in the Workplace for Learning, Innovation, and Growth. Hoboken, NJ: Wiley; 2018.
39. Huffington A. Thrive: The Third Metric to Redefining Success and Creating a Life of Well-Being, Wisdom, and Wonder. New York, NY: Harmony Books; 2014.
40. Susanna Schrobsdorff. Arianna Huffington on the Key to Finding Success (Without Burning Out). TIME [Internet]. 2014 Mar 24. Available from: https://time.com/36128/arianna-huffington-on-the-key-to-finding-success-without-burning-out/

41. Obama M. Becoming. New York, NY: Crown Publishing Group; 2018.

42. Laurence Paquette. Stop Negotiating With Myself. [LinkedIn] [Internet]. 2021. Available from: https://www.linkedin.com/pulse/stop-negotiating-myself-laurence-paquette-she-they-/?trackingId=u5FI%2BzVuSOmAOtvOwzmnUA%3D%3D

43. Park Y, Fritz C, Jex SM. Relationships between work-home segmentation and psychological detachment from work: The role of communication technology use at home. Journal of Applied Psychology. 2011;16(4):457–67.

44. Gallup. State of the Global Workplace 2022 Report [Internet]. Washington, D.C.: Gallup; 2022. Available from: https://www.gallup.com/workplace/349484/state-of-the-global-workplace.aspx

45. Bryant T. Homecoming: Overcome Fear and Trauma to Reclaim Your Whole Authentic Self. New York, NY: Tarcher Perigee; 2022.

46. Tawwab NG. Set Boundaries, Find Peace: A Guide to Reclaiming Yourself. New York, NY: Tarcher Perigee; 2021.

47. Rhimes S. Year of Yes: How to Dance It Out, Stand In the Sun and Be Your Own Person. New York, NY: Simon & Schuster; 2015.

48. Adam Grant. Give and Take: Why Helping Others Drives Our Success. Viking; 2013.

49. Maslach C, Leiter MP. The Truth About Burnout: How Organizations Cause Personal Stress and What to Do About It. San Francisco, CA: Jossey-Bass; 1997.

50. Jung CG. Two Essays on Analytical Psychology. Vol. 7. Princeton, NJ: Princeton University Press; 1966. (The Collected Works of CG Jung).

51. Eugene Kim. Yahoo CEO Marissa Mayer explains how she worked 130 hours a week and why it matters. Business Insider [Internet]. 2016 Aug 4. Available from: https://www.businessinsider.com/yahoo-ceo-marissa-mayer-on-130-hour-work-weeks-2016-8

52. World Health Organization. Burn-Out an "Occupational Phenomenon": International Classification of Diseases [Internet]. World Health Organization; 2019. Available from: https://www.who.int/news/item/28-05-2019-burn-out-an-occupational-phenomenon-international-classification-of-diseases

53. Knibbs K. Silicon Valley AI Startups Are Embracing China's Controversial '996' Work Schedule. Wired [Internet]. 2025 Jul. Available from: https://www.wired.com/story/silicon-valley-china-996-work-schedule/

54. Moss J. The Burnout Epidemic: The Rise of Chronic Stress and How We Can Fix It. Boston, MA: Harvard Business Review Press; 2021.

55. World Health Organization. Long Working Hours Increasing Deaths from Heart Disease and Stroke: WHO, ILO [Internet]. World Health Organization; 2021. Available from: https://www.who.int/news/item/17-05-2021-long-working-hours-increasing-deaths-from-heart-disease-and-stroke-who-ilo

56. Howard Schultz. Onward: How Starbucks Fought for Its Life without Losing Its Soul. New York, NY: Rodale Books; 2011.

57. Jiménez JM. The Burnout Fix: Overcome Overwhelm, Beat Busy, and Sustain Success in the New World of Work. New York, NY: McGraw Hill; 2021.

58. Gallup. State of the Global Workplace 2023 Report [Internet]. Gallup, Inc.; 2023. Available from: https://www.gallup.com/workplace/349484/state-of-the-global-workplace.aspx

59. Euro Health Net. Psychosocial Risks & Older Workers' Health [Internet]. 2022. Available from: https://eurohealthnet.eu/wp-content/uploads/publications/2022/221020_briefing_psychosocialstrategies.pdf

60. Swedish Social Insurance Agency (Försäkringskassan). Together for a Sustainable Working Life [Internet]. 2025. Available from: https://www.forsakringskassan.se/english/for-employers/together-for-a-sustainable-working-life

61. Mate G. The Myth of Normal: Trauma, Illness, and Healing in a Toxic Culture. New York, NY: Avery; 2022.

62. BBC NEWS. France brings in "right to disconnect" law. BBC News [Internet]. 2016. Available from: https://www.bbc.com/news/world-europe-38479439

63. France. Code du travail. Article L2242-17 (droit à la déconnexion). Code du travail. 2016.

64. Sandberg S. Option B: Facing Adversity, Building Resilience, and Finding Joy. New York, NY: Knopf; 2017.

65. Kübler-Ross E, Kessler D. On Grief and Grieving: Finding the Meaning of Grief Through the Five Stages of Loss. New York, NY: Scribner; 2005.

66. Kessler D. Finding Meaning: The Sixth Stage of Grief. New York, NY: Scribner; 2019.

67. Goleman D. What Makes a Leader? Harvard Business Review [Internet]. 2004. Available from: https://hbr.org/2004/01/what-makes-a-leader

68. Catmull E. Creativity, Inc.: Overcoming the Unseen Forces That Stand in the Way of True Inspiration. New York, NY: Random House; 2014.

69. Devine M. It's OK That You're Not OK: Meeting Grief and Loss in a Culture That Doesn't Understand. Boulder, CO: Sounds True; 2017.

70. Katie N. Hansen. Working Through Grief: Exploring the Relationship Between Organizational Support on Employee Engagement, Satisfaction and Loyalty. Transdisciplinary Journal of Management [Internet]. 2025. Available from: https://tjm.scholasticahq.com/article/142164-working-through-grief-exploring-the-relationship-between-organizational-support-on-employee-engagement-satisfaction-and-loyalty?utm_source=chatgpt.com

71. The Grief Recovery Institute. Grief in the Workplace [Internet]. 2017. Available from: https://www.griefrecoverymethod.com/blog/2017/07/grief-workplace

72. Adichie CN. Notes on Grief. London, UK: Fourth Estate; 2021.

73. Bonanno GA. The Other Side of Sadness: What the New Science of Bereavement Tells Us About Life After Loss. New York, NY: Basic Books; 2009.

74. O'Shea C. The Man from Zara: The Story of the Genius Behind the Inditex Group. London, UK: LID Publishing; 2012.

75. Encyclopaedia Britannica. Toni Morrison. In. Chicago: Encyclopaedia Britannica; 2026. Available from: https://www.britannica.com/biography/Toni-Morrison

76. Sanders H. Life as I Have Known It Has Been Finger Lickin' Good. Lexington, KY: University Press of Kentucky; 1974.

77. Encyclopaedia Britannica. Vera Wang. In. Chicago: Encyclopaedia Britannica; 2026. Available from: https://www.britannica.com/biography/Vera-Wang

78. Wang D, others. Hot Streaks in Artistic, Cultural, and Scientific Careers. Nature. 2018;559:396–9.

79. Azoulay P, et al. Age and High-Growth Entrepreneurship. American Economic Review: Insights. 2020;2(1):65–82.

80. Strauch B. The Secret Life of the Grown-Up Brain. New York, NY: Viking; 2010.

81. Price D. Unmasking Autism: Discovering the New Faces of Neurodiversity. New York, NY: Harmony Books; 2022.

82. Olivia B. Waxman. Grandma Moses Didn't Start Painting Until Her 70s. Here's Why. TIME [Internet]. 2016. Available from: https://time.com/4482257/grandma-moses-history/

83. Jane Ciabattari. Te-Ping Chen on Navigating Generational Difference and Political Turmoil. Literary Hub [Internet]. 2021. Available from: https://lithub.com/te-ping-chen-on-navigating-generational-difference-and-political-turmoil/?utm_source=chatgpt.com

84. Matthew Herskowitz. How Esther Perel Became the Modern Relationship Whisperer. GQ. 2025.

85. Davis V. Finding Me. New York, NY: HarperOne; 2022.

86. Thunberg G. No One Is Too Small to Make a Difference. London, UK: Penguin; 2019.

87. Ibarra H. Act Like a Leader, Think Like a Leader. Boston, MA: Harvard Business Review Press; 2015.

88. Ben Jacobs, Lauren Gambino. Democrats see major upset as socialist beats top-ranking US congressman. The Guardian [Internet]. 2018 Jun 27. Available from: https://www.theguardian.com/us-news/2018/jun/26/democrats-primaries-upset-joe-crowley-alexandria-osacio-cortez

89. Mohr T. Playing Big: Practical Wisdom for Women Who Want to Speak Up, Create, and Lead. New York, NY: Penguin Random House; 2014.

90. Lorde A. Sister Outsider: Essays and Speeches. Berkeley, CA: Crossing Press; 1984.

91. Duhigg C. What Google Learned From Its Quest to Build the Perfect Team [Internet]. The New York Times; 2016 Feb. Available from: https://www.nytimes.com/2016/02/28/magazine/what-google-learned-from-its-quest-to-build-the-perfect-team.html

92. Nanette. Los Gatos, CA: Netflix; 2018.

93. Charlotte Alter. How Whitney Wolfe Herd Turned a Vision of a Better Internet Into a Billion-Dollar Brand. TIME [Internet]. 2021 Mar 19. Available from: https://time.com/5947727/whitney-wolfe-herd-bumble/

94. Havel V. The Power of the Powerless. Armonk, NY: M.E. Sharpe; 1978.

95. Carney M. The Price of Silence: Remarks at the World Economic Forum Annual Meeting. 2026.

96. bell hooks. Feminist Theory: From Margin to Center. Boston, MA: South End Press; 1984.

97. Austin RD, Pisano GP. Neurodiversity as a Competitive Advantage. Harvard Business Review [Internet]. 2017. Available from: https://hbr.org/2017/05/neurodiversity-as-a-competitive-advantage

98. The Singing Revolution [Documentary]. Estonia; 2006.

99. Bandura A. Social Learning Theory. Englewood Cliffs, NJ: Prentice-Hall; 1977.

100. Foucault M. Discipline and Punish: The Birth of the Prison. New York, NY: Vintage Books; 1977.

101. Collins S. The Hunger Games. New York, NY: Scholastic Press; 2008.

102. Theoharis J. The Rebellious Life of Mrs. Rosa Parks. Beacon Press; 2013.

103. Yousafzai M, Lamb C. I Am Malala: The Girl Who Stood Up for Education and Was Shot by the Taliban. Little, Brown and Company; 2013.

104. Milano B. Taylor's Version of copyright. Harvard Law School [Internet]. 2024. Available from: https://hls.harvard.edu/today/how-taylor-swift-changed-the-copyright-game-by-remaking-her-own-music/

www.ingramcontent.com/pod-product-compliance
Lightning Source LLC
LaVergne TN
LVHW052123220926
848675LV00027B/293